Stand Fast Forever

A History of The English Evangelical Lutheran Church of the Holy Trinity and its 130 Years of Faith and Witness in the city of Buffalo, New York

by Martin J. Bauer

ISBN: 978-0-9841395-9-0
Library of Congress Control Number: 2013938784

Layout, cover, and design by BeauDesigns.

First Edition 2013.
Printed in the United States of America

Photographs are courtesy of the individual unless otherwise noted.

Every reasonable effort has been made to trace present copyright holders of the materials used in this book. Any omission is unintentional, and the author will be pleased to correct errors in future editions.

beau·
designs
www.BeauDesigns.biz

This book is dedicated to the memory of my father,
Rudolf L. Bauer,
Chairman of Holy Trinity's
125th anniversary celebration.

— Martin J. Bauer

A Note from the Author

*"Like Mount Zion, those who trust in the Lord
stand fast forever...."*

(adapted from Psalm 125)

In the autumn of 2004, Pastor Eva Steege returned to Holy Trinity to preach during our church's 125th anniversary celebration. After the 10:30am service, I visited with Eva in the parish conference room, and told her that I was working on a history of Holy Trinity. Eva was pleased to hear this and told me that she had attended a seminar where it was said that every congregation has its "DNA." Eva's recollection was like a proverbial lightning bolt to me. It became the theme around which this book is written and the rich, faith – filled history it recounts.

The title of this book, "Stand Fast Forever," is adapted from a verse in Psalm 125. This scripture, to me, evokes strength — the strength found in the faith of the Holy Trinity congregation throughout its 130 year history. This strong faith founded a parish, moved forward with worship in the English language, built a permanent sanctuary on Main Street in Buffalo, New York, reached across the country and the globe to touch many lives while accomplishing great work within its own walls and its own community.

This Lutheran congregation showed its strength when calling clergy to the pulpit of this church – only 6 senior pastors in 130 years! Strength, too, describes those six voices in the pulpit and the gifts they have given the faithful in this place of worship.

Finally, strength is what God has given this congregation through the creative and redemptive love of Jesus Christ. God has given the people of Holy Trinity a strong faith in the good times, that same strength in the challenging times, and a strong vision of what had to be done at each turn in the history of this parish.

Here are some notes I would like to impart about the writing of this book. The history of Holy Trinity from 1879 through 1979 contained in this volume has been taken from "An Historical Sketch of The Holy Trinity Church" by Frederick Henrich, published in 1937, and "This Faith Tremendous" by Dr. Ralph Loew, Mrs. Kenneth Eckhert, Sr., and David M. Hehr, published for the Main Street church's 100th anniversary in 1979. This book is meant to be faithful to and seen as a continuation of those works. It should be noted that some biographical references in part two were adapted by me from "A Short Biography of Frederick Kahler, D.D., L.D.D." by Paul Bloomhardt, PhD.- also published in the same volume as the 1937 Henrich history of Holy Trinity. You, the reader, should know that the voices of these authors still live in this book, and you may hear them in the turn of a phrase or a sentence that is used.

One final bibliographic note: I have used quotes from local Buffalo newspapers to make alive certain events and moments in the life of Holy Trinity. This is especially true with regard to episodes that happened in the first fifty years of the Main Street church. By using the observations of journalists of those earlier times, I felt that events seen through their eyes might yet still "live." Citations of these quotes are built into the text in order to properly credit their sources.

The history I have compiled of Holy Trinity from 1980 to the present has been taken from issues of "Our Church Paper" from the aforementioned period of time, recollections from Pastor Charles D. Bang and Organist and Choirmaster James Bigham, and observations from my 26 years as a member of this parish.

As you read this history, you will notice the use of hymn lyrics. First, each chapter begins with words from hymns that symbolize each pastor. The lyrics at the beginning of the Loew, Winters, and Bang years come from the favorite hymns of each of these clergymen. All hymn lyrics used in this book come from <u>Lutheran Book of Worship</u> published by Augsburg Publishing House, Minneapolis, Minnesota, copyright 1978.

Finally, I wish to thank all those who helped me in the journey of writing this book. First, I would like to thank Frederick Henrich, Dr. Paul Bloomhardt, Dr.Ralph Loew, Mrs. Kenneth Eckhert, Sr., and David Hehr for writing their previous histories of Holy Trinity. Thanks to the five of you for beginning the historical record of this church and building the foundation for this book.

Second, thank you to all who have written, edited, and contributed to "Our Church Paper." I want all who read this book to remember that this publication is both Holy Trinity's congregational communication tool, and our own historical record. I have found this newspaper to be invaluable for this book — especially for compiling the Winters and Bang years. Thank you to David Schopp and the Renovation Committee of the 1990's for their detailed reports in "Our Church Paper." These articles helped to shape the story of a great and challenging project in Holy Trinity's history.

A great, big thank you to Mr. Martin Wright for typing this manuscript. I filled somewhere in the neighborhood of at least four legal pads when writing the initial draft of this book. Marty took each installment and recreated it in cyberspace. I cannot thank you enough, Marty, for your help!

Many thanks go to Pastor Charles Bang for his help with historical references, and his guidance and assistance with the preparation of this book.

Getting this project across "the finish line" was a challenging task. I want to thank Millie Nikischer for getting this book to the final phase of preparation. A giant thank you must be given to Gail Camilleri and the Holy Trinity Publication Committee for spending countless hours proofreading the final draft of this book and for helping to choose the photographs that have been included in the text. My thanks to the Publication Committee members, Karen Saona, Carole Casterline, and Herbert Hough for all their help. Thank you to Amy Freiermuth of BeauDesigns, graphic design, printing and publishing for doing the final layout and formatting the book. Finally a heartfelt thank you to Pastor Neil Kattermann for his enthusiasm for and encouragement of this project in its final phase.

I would like to offer a huge thank you to my family for their help and support during this entire project. Thank you to my father, Rudy, for his motivation and encouragement. Thank you to my mother, Julie, who, after Dad passed away, continued the motivation and created some great "writer's workshops." And my thanks and love to my wife, Mary Sue

Bauer, for her love, support, and encouragement with this book. Mary Sue helped me with the editing and proofreading of the manuscript; her assistance with this part of the project was invaluable.

Finally, my thanks to God for watching over me and guiding me through this project. Thank you, Lord, for all your blessings — through the journey of writing this history, and throughout my fifty-one years.

The fifth verse of Psalm 46 reads: "God is in the midst of the city . . ." The beautiful Lutheran church near the intersection of Main and North Streets in Buffalo, New York with its "faith tremendous" is a testament to the truth of this scripture. It has truly been an honor for me to tell its story!

— Martin J. Bauer

Part One: The Beginning

"A mighty fortress is our God
A sword and shield victorious;
He breaks the cruel oppressor's rod
And wins salvation glorious . . ."

Martin Luther
LBW Hymn 229

The year was 1879. The United States was moving toward a new century. Rutherford B. Hayes was the American President, and two states, California and Louisiana, celebrated the ratification of their constitutions. In 1879, Thomas Edison perfected the first practical incandescent light bulb. In Utica, New York, F. W. Woolworth opened the first five and ten cent store. Ivory, the first floating soap, was introduced by Proctor and Gamble. In the same year, across the Atlantic Ocean, life dawned on Albert Einstein and Joseph Stalin – both of whom would leave their indelible marks on the century to come.

In 1879, Buffalo, New York was in its most prosperous period. Buoyed by post-Civil War industrial expansion, Buffalo was in what some have termed the "Gilded Age." In a publication for the Buffalo and Erie County Historical Society, historian Olga Lindberg describes Buffalo as a community where "large comfortable mansions lined the tree-shaded avenues and parkways with small brick and frame homes along the side streets." Lindberg goes on to say that Buffalo became a fine residential city thanks to its parks, churches, theaters, libraries, museums, and a progressive school system. At the same time, Buffalo was a hub of rail and shipping activity, and industries such as lumber, iron, foundries, and breweries were growing rapidly and achieving success. All in all, in the 1870s Buffalo, New York was one of America's most progressive cities.

Against that backdrop, on May 5, 1879, a group of bold German Lutherans made manifest that which had first been a vision: they held the first regular congregational meeting of their new English Evangelical Lutheran Church. The determined individuals who gathered this particular evening had one goal in mind: to worship God in the English language.

In 1875, there were six Lutheran congregations in Buffalo; four of these worshipped in German, one in Norwegian, and one in French. The staunch German Lutheran residents of the city were firm in their belief that German must be the language used in their worship services. They said: "Englisch ist fur gelt gemachen; Deutsch ist zum beten." Translated this means: "English is to make money with; German is to pray with." During the Advent season of 1878, however, winds of change had begun to make their presence felt in Buffalo Lutheranism.

There had been debates about whether worship services should be in German and other languages or in English. The Civil War, however, delayed the answer to this question. In 1878, a group of "liberals" asked Rev. Levi H. Geshwind of Pittsburgh, Pennsylvania to come to Western

New York to discuss the possibility of beginning Lutheran work in the city of Buffalo.

In his memoirs, Andrew Kurtz, a member of the first congregational council reflected on the "exploratory" meetings in 1878 about Lutheran work in English. He wrote:

> *"Gustav Kleindinst invited the Rev. Geshwind to come to Buffalo to look over the field, suggest the forming of an English Lutheran congregation, and to aid in its beginning. He directed the Reverend Geshwind to the home of his father-in-law, Mr. Phillip Becker. These few went to the office of Mr. Henry Koons. Mr. Koons was heartily in favor of the undertaking and directed us to Mr. James Schneider, a trustee of the French Protestant Church, to ascertain if the church building could be used for services on the following Sunday."*

The first Holy Trinity Lutheran Church located at Ellicott and Tupper Streets.

Part One: The Beginning

Reverend Geshwind was, indeed, extended a call to become pastor of the new congregation, and on December 15, 1878, that small, staunch, and devoted band of laymen held services in the facilities of the French Protestant Church which they had rented at the corner of Ellicott and Tupper Streets. During that day, those present pledged $606 toward the salary of their first pastor. A meeting was held that same evening in the choir loft of the French church. Twenty-eight were in attendance and they discussed ways of financing a new English Lutheran church. It is important to note that on that third Sunday in Advent, those devoted parishioners began a tradition of a self-supporting congregation which has never received funds from other agencies.

On May 5, 1879, a congregational meeting took place with sixty-seven members in attendance. A constitution was signed, and William Hengerer, a successful local businessman, was elected president of the congregation. Hengerer, who was the son of a Lutheran minister, came to Buffalo in 1861 from Pittsburgh, Pennsylvania. He began his career as a clerk in the dry goods business of Sherman, Barnes, and Company. His ability enabled him to eventually head the local store, William Hengerer and Co., which would be

William Hengerer, first president of the congregation of Holy Trinity.

Louisa Hengerer, wife of William, president of the first Women's Society of Holy Trinity.

named after him in 1895. It was William Hengerer who had been one of the main visionaries of English Lutheranism in Buffalo. It was he who believed a congregation could be formed and was willing to back it with his resources and influence. Now, he was elected the leader of the congregation he had envisioned, and the English Lutheranism he foresaw had truly begun.

By October of 1879, the congregation of Holy Trinity continued its organization by forming a women's society with twelve charter members. Louisa Hengerer, wife of William, was elected president of this group.

By 1881, the first English Lutheran congregation in Buffalo became legally recognized. On May 24 of that year, the certificate of incorporation of "The English Evangelical Lutheran Church of the Holy Trinity" was filed. On September 27, 1881, the consolidation of the First French Protestant Church with Holy Trinity Lutheran became effective. As a result, many families of the French Protestant Church joined the new congregation. The year concluded with the premises at Ellicott and Tupper Streets being conveyed by deed to Holy Trinity on November 10. Eighteen eighty-one had indeed been a busy yet fruitful year for the new Lutheran church.

Part One: The Beginning

In the 1979 history of Holy Trinity, the first few years in the life of the church were characterized as follows:

"This beginning had all the marks of success. Yet, Mrs. Eliza Haller, who lived to be 106 years of age, used to say that she had been among those original persons forming the church but did not sign the charter, preferring, as she said, with a twinkle in her eye, 'to wait and see if anything came of it.'"

Something, indeed, <u>was</u> coming of the new church. By 1884, the congregation of the first English Evangelical Lutheran Church in Buffalo had grown to 131 members with 149 registered in the Sunday School. After five years, that bold group of German Lutherans who had desired to worship God in the English language had become a bright new hope in a rapidly growing city.

Pastor Levi Geshwind knew that in those same five years, that which had been an exciting vision was now alive and growing. Pastor Geshwind had formed an English Lutheran congregation that had a promising future. Believing that he had accomplished his mission, Pastor Geshwind resigned from his position at Holy Trinity on February 14, 1884. With the departure of its first pastor, the small congregation of Holy Trinity Lutheran Church was confronted with a difficult decision: after five years of foundation-building, they would have to call a new pastor.

Reverend Levi H. Geshwind, the first pastor of Holy Trinity, 1879

Part Two: The Kahler Years

"Holy, holy, holy Lord God Almighty
Early in the morning
our song shall rise to thee.
Holy, holy, holy, merciful and mighty
God in three Persons
blessed Trinity!"

LBW 165

The spring and fall of 1884 were probably exciting and uncertain periods in the life of Holy Trinity. During that time, calls were sent to three different pastors – each of whom refused the offer to shepherd the young progressive English Lutheran congregation in the city of Buffalo.

According to Dr. Paul Bloomhardt, the resignation of Pastor Geshwind brought discouragement to the small church at Ellicott and Tupper. That all changed when a call was extended to Frederick August Kahler to become the second pastor of the English Evangelical Lutheran Church of the Holy Trinity.

The thirty-four-year-old pastor, born September 21, 1850, had grown up in Erie, Pennsylvania, and received most of his education in Montreal, where his father had been serving as a pastor. After leaving Canada, Frederick Kahler came to Western New York. He settled in Dansville,

New York, and became both vice president and an instructor at the Dansville Seminary. It is interesting to note that Frederick Kahler was only nineteen years of age at the time.

Two years into his tenure in Dansville, the young teacher chose to answer his true calling. Dr. Paul Bloomhardt, in his 1937 biography of Dr. Kahler, wrote:

> *"In his twenty-first year his circumstances made it possible for him to turn again to the path which his deepest desires inclined him to follow. These desires were for the Christian ministry."*

Margaretha Kahler Henrich, when commenting about her father's faith journey, said: "For him to live was Christ." In 1871, Frederick Kahler enrolled at the Theological Seminary in Philadelphia and then served St. Michael's Lutheran Church which was located near the campus where he had prepared for his ministry.

Reverend Frederick A. Kahler, the second pastor of Holy Trinity, 1884

On August 5, 1879, Pastor Frederick Kahler was married to Miss Margaret Torbert McNair whom he had met while serving as a teacher in Dansville. In 1883, the young pastor, still at St. Michael's, received a job offer to teach at Gustavus Adolphus College in Minnesota. He turned the offer down. In 1884,

Pastor Kahler received an offer to chair the English and Philosophy Department at Augustana College in Illinois. He turned this prestigious position down as well. It was then that he received calls to two of the only three English Lutheran churches of the General Council in the state of New York. Frederick Kahler accepted the most challenging of the two: Holy Trinity Lutheran Church in Buffalo.

On October 15, 1884, Frederick August Kahler officially became the second pastor of Holy Trinity Lutheran Church. At the time Dr. Kahler arrived, there were only 131 in the congregation. Under his leadership, the church and its mission in the city of Buffalo would be energized and grow rapidly.

Two years into his ministry at Holy Trinity, Dr. Kahler knew that the work of his church had to go beyond the walls of the building at Ellicott and Tupper. In 1886, he encouraged Sunday School teachers from Holy Trinity to open a branch Sunday School. The Sunday School extension was created in a cottage on Eagle Street. This took place because much more had to be done in the area of Sunday School work at Holy Trinity.

In his historical sketch of Holy Trinity from 1937, Frederick Henrich writes that under Dr. Kahler's leadership " . . . the work assumed new proportions, both congregation and Sunday School growing rapidly. The progress was steady and strong. . . . " So steady was the growth of the congregation that by 1887, the little church building at Ellicott and Tupper had to be enlarged. An extension was built at the formidable sum of $8,000 in order to provide space for many new Sunday School classes and a new pipe organ. During this time, a music program – one that would become very significant in the life of Holy Trinity - was begun as the church formed both mens and boys choirs.

Another step in the growth of Holy Trinity took place in 1891 with the publication of the first issue of *Our Church Paper*. Louis Bergtold, an active participant of the Sunday School, suggested the establishment of the publication. It was started by a member of the parish who was a printer. The following editorial comment appeared in the December 1891 issue of *Our Church Paper*. It offers an "alternative" view of the process of worship:

"The services are attended by increasing numbers, but the increase should be larger. We know that the numbers do not make the proper spirit of the service, but the proper spirit in the hearts of the people will bring the numbers."

As of the publication of this book, 122 years later, *Our Church Paper* continues to be an important tool of communication within Holy Trinity Church.

The 1890s could easily be called the "outreach" decade in Holy Trinity's history. As he had done in the mid-1880s, Dr. Kahler once again extended the church's influence in the city of Buffalo beyond its own walls. On May 1, 1893, at its annual meeting, the congregation of Holy Trinity authorized its trustees to purchase a property on Eagle Street west of Jefferson Avenue. By February of 1894, a building stood on the lot that had been purchased only ten months before! Thus, Holy Trinity began a satellite location in which was created an outreach ministry.

In the same year activity began at the Eagle Street location, another satellite was taking off. The branch Sunday School begun in 1886 had grown so rapidly that the group that first inhabited a cottage on Eagle Street rented the nearby Swedish Lutheran Church on Spring Street. By 1894, the Sunday School had grown into a congregation which was organized as The Church of the Atonement one year later.

During this time, the city of Buffalo continued to grow with its west side attracting much attention. Spacious houses on handsome, tree-lined avenues such as Delaware, Elmwood and Richmond became the residences of the affluent. Since many of Holy Trinity's leaders now lived in this area, it was decided that another satellite congregation could be formed. In a spirit typical of his ministry, Dr. Kahler led the effort to establish this outreach opportunity. On December 16, 1894, the Holy Trinity congregation resolved to buy the Presbyterian Church of the Redeemer at the corner of Elmwood and Highland Avenue for a sum of $14,250. The name "Church of the Redeemer" was adopted and nine of twelve deacons from Holy Trinity joined this entity.

Some of the deacons assumed that Dr. Kahler would come with them to the new church on the affluent west side. He surprised them, apparently, remaining with the "mother church" on Ellicott Street.

During this busy, fruitful, and creative time in the mid-1890s, Holy Trinity continued to influence life in Buffalo. In 1896, Mrs. Kahler, wife of the pastor, conceived the idea for a church-sponsored nursing home in the city. Dr. Kahler and members of Holy Trinity took up the concept and, with other Lutheran parishes in Buffalo, established "The Lutheran Church Home For The Aged and Infirm." With Holy Trinity's leadership, this institution would evolve and grow for years to come.

Even though there were two other English Lutheran

parishes in the vicinity of Holy Trinity, the number of parishioners in the pews of the small building on Ellicott Street continued to increase. It was because of this that the greatest change in the life of the congregation was about to happen. On May 3, 1897, at the annual meeting of the church, the matter of a new sanctuary for the vibrant congregation was first "put on the table" for discussion. It was clear that Holy Trinity was outgrowing its present location. Furthermore, a conviction was evolving that a great central "cathedral" for the English Lutheran movement needed to be built.

A committee was then appointed to explore the issue of a larger sanctuary for the Holy Trinity congregation. Henry Koons, a member of the first Church Council was made the chairman. Other members included John Ansteth, Andrew J. Kurtz, Christian W. Schaefer, Menno A. Reeb, Louis Bergtold, Frederick Henrich, and Dr. Kahler.

After exploring several possibilities for the location of the new sanctuary, including the vicinity of Elmwood and Highland Avenues, where some of the strength of the church had gone, it was decided that this central church should be built not far away from the current Ellicott and Tupper location. On September 5, 1899, an option was taken on a lot located on Main Street near North Street. This piece of land had 110 feet of frontage and 217 feet in depth and was currently home to an orchard. One newspaper account termed the lot "one of the choicest pieces of realty on upper Main Street." On October 30, 1899, the congregation of Holy Trinity bought the lot at a cost of $26,675. The architectural firm of Lansing and Beierl was then hired to design plans for the new central church. As the nineteenth century drew to a close, the family of Holy Trinity had much to look forward to. Buoyed by strong faith and great optimism, this burgeoning congregation was standing on the threshold of the next important step in the growth of English Lutheranism in the city of Buffalo.

In the 1979 history of Holy Trinity, Dr. Ralph Loew writes,

"One can imagine the excitement....when the plans for the new building were displayed in the little church on Ellicott Street."

These plans were put on display and adopted by the congregation in January, 1903. One of the architects, a Roman Catholic, decided that since Protestants must listen to sermons during their services, there would be no columns or obstructions in the nave of the new church. Instead, the English Gothic structure was designed with a double ceiling, and the weight was supported by steel trusses.

On March 18, 1903, contracts for the new building were signed totaling $106,402.16. One month later, Holy Trinity was granted a $70,000 mortgage on its lot at Main and North Streets. The project of building a central English Lutheran church was now gaining momentum, and the time had come for a ground breaking.

The Buffalo Times of April 21, 1903 reported:

".... In the center of an old orchard on a beautiful site, between North and St. Paul Streets on the north side of Main Street, several hundred parishioners of the English Evangelical Lutheran Church gathered today to witness the ceremony of breaking ground for their new church building...."

Part Two: The Kahler Years

Before the first shovelful of earth was turned, Pastor Kahler opened the ceremony with a few remarks. He said that upon that spot great trees had once reared their heads to shelter the red man of the forest, that an orchard had been planted to nourish the white man, and now, a church was about to be planted to scatter blessings to all mankind. Then, Pastor Kahler brought forward Henry Koons, chairman of the Building Committee, and asked him to turn the first spade of earth. It should be noted that one of those who broke ground that April day was Christian F. Fifer. *The Buffalo Times* described Mr. Fifer as "the oldest man in the congregation, he being 79 years of age . . . ."

Lansing and Beierl, the architects, expected to have the new sanctuary ready for occupancy during the spring of 1904. The auditorium of the building would have the capability to seat about 1000 people and the Sunday School, about 900 people. The entire structure would be heated with hot water and would have lights powered by electricity.

Members of Holy Trinity's congregation hoped that their new church would be ready at the time estimated by the architects. One newspaper article during April of 1903 speculated that due to the great nature of the project, that hope might not be realized. Sure enough, something unexpected did slow construction.

In June, 1903, a dispute developed between the stonecutters and stonemasons unions over the work involved in building the new church. A newspaper account from *The Buffalo Commercial* of November 13, 1903 described the conflict:

"It developed that each union claimed that the other union infringed upon its particular line of work...."

Architectural illustration from 1903 of the new Holy Trinity Lutheran Church to be built on Main Street in Buffalo.

It took five months to settle the dispute. After the problem was put to rest, some members of Holy Trinity suggested that work on the new sanctuary be completely stopped until the spring of 1904. They felt that members of both unions ought to be punished for not working when work was available.

Construction of the new sanctuary of Holy Trinity Church resumed in November 1903 with a push to complete the project as soon as possible. A big event in the life of the congregation took place on the afternoon of December 13, 1903 with the laying of the cornerstone of the new Evangelical Lutheran Church of the Holy Trinity.

Delayed by the labor dispute that lingered from June through October of 1903, the ceremony took place on a bit-

Part Two: The Kahler Years

ORDER OF SERVICE

AT THE

Laying of the Corner-stone

OF THE

ENGLISH LUTHERAN CHURCH

OF THE HOLY TRINITY.

Main St.,   Opposite St. Paul St.

BUFFALO, N. Y.

DECEMBER 13, 1903, at 3 P. M.

F. A. Kähler, D. D., Pastor.

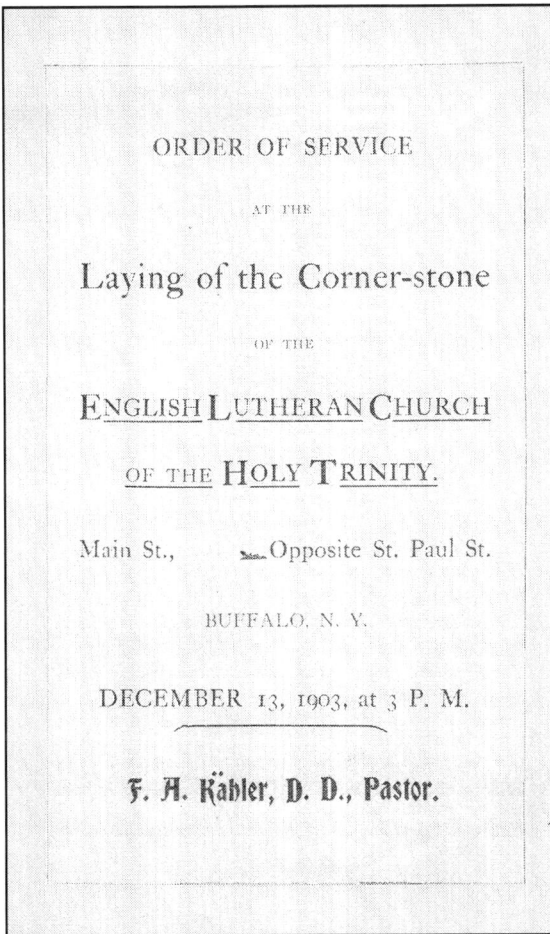

Cover of the bulletin published for the laying of Holy Trinity's cornerstone in December of 1903.

ter cold afternoon. Dr. Kahler sent announcements to members of the congregation to be "on hand punctually" at 3 o'clock in the afternoon as he would begin the cornerstone service on time and would end it as soon as possible.

In spite of the uncomfortble weather conditions, there was excitement surrounding the ceremony in the freezing, windswept Main Street orchard. In *The Buffalo Courier* newspaper account of December 14, 1903, the headline read:

". . . . In Bitter Cold, Scores of Loyal and Enthusiastic Parishoners of English Lutheran Church Attend Cornerstone Laying...."

Due to the bitter cold, the service was rushed. The tradition of music accenting significant events in the life of the church was further solidified by the presence of the church choir. These faithful servants were heavily bundled in cloaks and coats. According to *The Buffalo Courier* article, the choir members' ". . . throats were muffled against the biting wind." The ceremony was kept simple. The choir sang a hymn. Then, Dr. Kahler led a responsive reading with the congregation. After Dr. Kahler offered a prayer, a huge white Medina sandstone block was slowly lowered into its place.

Toward the end of the ceremony, Dr. Kahler said a few words of congratulations and thanks for the success which had crowned the efforts of Lutheran worship in English in the city of Buffalo. And a crowning achievement this was as the laying of the white Medina cornerstone was the next big step in the construction of a cathedral church for English Lutheranism in Western New York. The new sanctuary would not be ready for another 16 months, but the anticipation of its completion continued to energize the hopeful congregation.

In 1904, the New York Central Railroad published a series of travel brochures which described major stops along its route. In Volume Number 38 titled "Buffalo and Niagara Falls – The Coming Industrial Center of the United States," a description of religious venues seems to capture the placement of Holy Trinity Lutheran Church on Main Street:

> *". . . The churches are not only architecturally attractive, but in every case there has been a happy choice of location where their graceful outlines are not hidden by near-by dwellings. . . ."*

Part Two: The Kahler Years

The new sanctuary of Holy Trinity would be no exception. Over one hundred years later, the graceful, proud visage of the English Evangelical Lutheran Church is still visible to all who pass by as they travel Main Street.

The last services in the building at Ellicott and Tupper Streets took place on April 9, 1905. In *The Buffalo Commercial Newspaper* of April 10, 1905, it was reported that more than 500 attended the last service, and "every seat was occupied and many were standing." The same article indicates that the "old" Holy Trinity building would soon be remodeled into a carriage factory. Even though the services of Holy Trinity would soon continue in a beautiful new sanctuary, the turn-of-the-century journalist still laments the change coming over the old building:

"By the noise of workmen and machinery, the sacred quiet which has brooded over the place for a quarter of a century will be driven out into the modern hustling world. The pulpit and chancel, where deaths have been mourned, births rejoiced, and marriages solemnized will be stripped of the dignity endowed upon them by these momentous occasions."

Five days later, in the same *Buffalo Commercial* newspaper, a headline read:

"HANDSOME CHURCH. . . . New Home of English Lutheran Church of the Holy Trinity is Finished"

The first service in the new sanctuary of Holy Trinity Lutheran Church was held on Palm Sunday of 1905. It was attended by 1507 persons who were both in the church and its vestibules. On this day, Dr. Kahler commenced his sermon with words that had been spoken before a small congregation at the first Holy Trinity Church at Ellicott and Tupper twenty-seven years earlier:

> **"Sing unto the Lord a new song, for he has triumphed gloriously . . . ."**

The Buffalo Evening News reported that in his sermon, Dr. Kahler "drew a parallel between the children of Israel crossing the Red Sea, and the congregation present. He told them that although beset by difficulties, the church had prospered beyond the most sanguine expectation. When referring to the history, he remarked on the many blessings that had been received."

The large window in the sanctuary given to Holy Trinity in 1905 by Dr. Eugene Smith in memory of his two children.

Part Two: The Kahler Years

By the following Sunday, Easter 1905, a large window in the sanctuary dedicated to the Sunday School was completed. Given by Dr. Eugene Smith in memory of his two children, the design in the window is a depiction of Christ blessing little children. One hundred and four years later, this gift to Holy Trinity can still be seen not far from the church's baptismal font.

On the morning of May 7, 1905, one headline in *The Buffalo Courier* proclaimed: "New Church To Be Consecrated." It was the 26th anniversary of The English Evangelical Lutheran Church of the Holy Trinity and quite an observance and celebration was planned. The consecration of the new church began on Sunday morning, May 7, at 10:45 a.m. Dr. Kahler and the officers of the congregation entered through the front door in a procession commencing the first of five services to be held in the space of three days. On that first day of consecration, additional worship services were held at 3 pm and 8 pm.

On Monday evening, May 8, 1905, a fourth service was

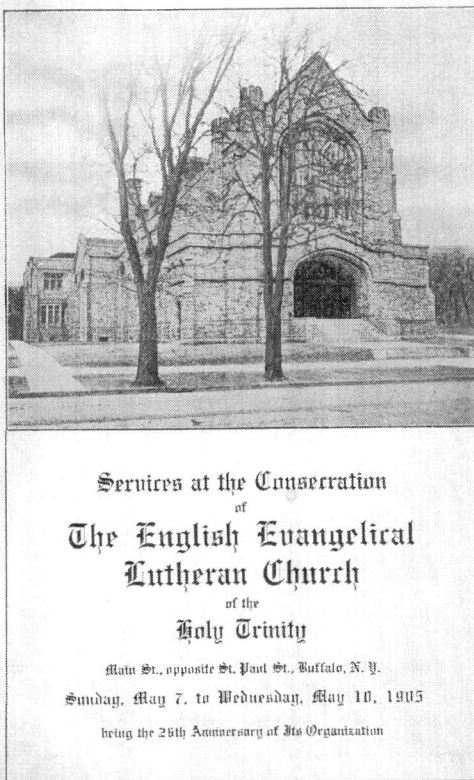

Services at the Consecration
of
The English Evangelical
Lutheran Church
of the
Holy Trinity

Main St., opposite St. Paul St., Buffalo, N. Y.

Sunday, May 7, to Wednesday, May 10, 1905

being the 26th Anniversary of Its Organization

The cover of the bulletin for services at the consecration of the new Holy Trinity Church in 1905.

held. This one was dedicated to Holy Trinity's Sunday School. On Tuesday evening, May 9, the last worship service in the observance was held at Holy Trinity. Its focus was on the organizations of the church. A look at the bulletin for the consecration events indicates that two sermons were given. One was dedicated to young people's work; the other was about women's work in the church.

The final event in the consecration of Holy Trinity's new sanctuary was on Wednesday, May 10, 1905. It was a reception planned by a committee of 10 women led by Mrs. Kahler, the pastor's wife. Held at 8 o'clock in the evening in the parish hall below the sanctuary, the event was attended by about 1,000 people. According to an article in *The Buffalo Courier* of May 11, 1905, the room where the reception took place was decorated with cherry blossoms, and eleven women of the church served refreshments.

The consecration events at Holy Trinity were very well attended and received. The church had five worship services in four days, nine guest pastors (including the Rev. J. A. W. Haas, who was the president of Muhlenberg College), and a large reception. Another look at the consecration bulletin reveals that music, one of Holy Trinity's strongest traditions, was ever present. The Holy Trinity choir sang three anthems; there were four solo pieces sung by four different soloists, and a piece sung at the last service by a guest quartet from Holy Trinity's "daughter" congregation, The Church of the Redeemer. The congregation of Holy Trinity contributed musically as well. Over the five worship services in three days, fourteen hymns were sung by those attending worship.

It must be noted that at the service on Sunday, May 7, 1905, at 3pm, two addresses were given, and both, ironically, were in German. The second address in German was followed by a hymn: the congregation sang "A Mighty Fortress is Our God" in English. It is interesting to consider that there would not be another address in German at Holy Trinity until 1976.

Finally, many special gifts and memorials given by congregation members were dedicated during the consecration of the new sanctuary. Henry Koons, chairman of the Building Committee, gave the altar and reredos, the altar rail and mosaic floor, the bronze lectern, the pulpit, the electric fixtures, and the wiring. Other gifts from the congregation included the organ (given by the Women's Society); the pastor's robe and study; the Bibles for the pulpit and lectern; hymnals for the chancel; an altar vase and brass altar desk; the brass offering plates; the central lancet of the large front window; three windows in the sanctuary; and the furnishings of the secretary's room, the Sunday School, and the parish house. As the congregation of Holy Trinity had so generously given what was needed to build a new cathedral church for English Lutheranism in Buffalo, the same giving spirit made the sanctuary ready for worship. In time, the congregation would be called on to give again, and the response would be the same: the family of Holy Trinity always accomplished its objective by using its own resources – all for the glory of God.

The congregation of Holy Trinity had much to celebrate at its anniversary in May, 1905. In twenty-six years, the congregation had raised almost $214,000, founded two branch congregations, bought a Main Street lot, and built a cathedral church on that land. Its pastor, Dr. Frederick Kahler, since accepting his call in 1884, had received almost 2500 members into the church with the present membership in 1905 being about 1400. A quotation from a newspaper story of the day sums it all up: "There is an expansiveness about it all that is very impressive and at the same time there is a comfortable coziness that is readily enjoyed. That is Holy Trinity Evangelical Lutheran Church, and may she continue to flourish as she always has in the past. . . ." In May of 1906, the committee responsible for building the new sanctuary gave its final report at the annual meeting of the congregation. They announced that the final cost of the new church building was $148,799.16.

The extension of English Lutheran congregation-building continued as the new sanctuary of Holy Trinity was being constructed. In 1903, Holy Trinity united with the Church of the Atonement and the Church of the Redeemer to begin Grace Lutheran Church in South Buffalo. In 1906, the same three churches helped to organize Grace Lutheran Church in North Tonawanda, New York. With five English Lutheran congregations now organized in Western New York, an English Conference of the General Council was formed in order to further unify the growing English Lutheran witness in the area. The English Conference chose Holy Trinity as its meeting place in 1907.

In 1909, Holy Trinity celebrated its 30th anniversary. In an announcement in *The Buffalo Courier* of May 1, 1909, the celebration of three decades of witness in Buffalo included an anniversary sermon by Dr. Kahler and "special music by the vested choir." Once again, music was planned to accent a special event in the life of the congregation. During the same year Holy Trinity marked another milestone in its history, the Laymen's Missionary Movement was sweeping across the United States – its beginning taking place in Buffalo in October of 1909. In January of 1910, the Men's Bible Class entered the movement by undertaking the task of providing support of Reverend C. F. Kuder as a missionary to India. Once again, in order to make an impact within their church, members of Holy Trinity looked beyond the walls of their sanctuary.

Holy Trinity, along with the Church of the Atonement and the Church of the Redeemer, continued to build English Lutheranism in Buffalo. In 1911, these three congregations started the Church of the Resurrection at Genesee and Doat Streets. The following year, an opportunity came about to rent the church building at the corner of Amherst and Fairfield Streets in the Central Park region of Buffalo. It would become known as Parkside Lutheran Church.

While Holy Trinity continued the extension of English Lutheran work in Western New York, much activity was going on within the walls of the Main Street sanctuary. The Sunday School, Men's Group, and Women's Society all continued to grow and were active in the life of the parish. As Dr. Ralph Loew put it in the 1979 history of Holy Trinity: "All of this congregational activity meant that increased administrative detail demanded additional professional leadership." By now, Dr. Kahler was 63 years old, and had recently chosen not to run for re-election as president of the English Synod to which Holy Trinity belonged. He cited both health issues and, in the words of Dr. Paul Bloomhardt, "his overwhelming obligations in Buffalo."

Holy Trinity had called assistant pastors before, but they had both been assigned the task of developing the two daughter churches during the 1890s. In 1913, Holy Trinity extended a call to Reverend W. Karl Hemsath to become its own first assistant pastor. In the 100 years that have followed, there has always been more than one pastor on staff at Holy Trinity.

In 1913, another change came in the day-to-day activity of the church. Renting of pews was abolished and the plan of giving through pledges and envelopes was instituted.

Through all the changes, extensions, building, and growing, Dr. Kahler continued to be devoted to one role in the church: being a parish pastor. A side note in the 100th Anniversary history of Holy Trinity describes the activity surrounding the annual Sunday School picnic. Parishioners would board a train at the New York Central Railroad station on Exchange Street which would then take them to a local park. On the way, Dr. Kahler would walk through each railroad passenger car and greet the congregation members on board. Later, Dr. Kahler would often act as umpire of the baseball game between the ushers and the Luther League members. Yachting parties were also very popular at Holy Trinity. As usual, Dr. Kahler would greet all those on board. He would also be the first off the boat at journey's end to bid all a good night.

In 1914, a Women's Bible Class was started at Holy Trinity. Another significant change in worship was made by the church that same year as Holy Trinity adopted use of the individual cup for Communion.

Over the years, national and international events would touch the life of the congregation and the lives within it. The First World War broke out in Europe in 1914 and its effects would be felt at Holy Trinity. As the 1979 history of the church states, "An enormous anti-German feeling swept the nation, outlawing the teaching of German in schools. German books were burned in public places and

A photograph of Reverend Kahler and his wife taken in the latter part of his ministry at Holy Trinity

a militant nationalism was everywhere. Despite the fact that Holy Trinity had always used English in its worship services and in its activities, it was still a very difficult time for Dr. Kahler and many members whose cultural rootage was in Europe." Ultimately, the war would bring 156 men of Holy Trinity into active service. Six of these made the supreme sacrifice as they perished in battle.

Some months after the war ended, Dr. Kahler was stricken with a serious illness. He had to have surgery after which his recovery was slow. According to his biographer, Dr. Kahler "never fully regained his vigor." Life went on, though, at Holy Trinity. In 1919, the church celebrated its 40th Anniversary. By that year, the mortgage on the Main Street building of Holy Trinity had been reduced to $29,000. At a congregational meeting on March 11, 1919, it was decided that a concerted effort needed to be made to wipe out the mortgage debt. As Frederick Henrich states in his 1937 history of Holy Trinity, this would be "a thank offering in observance of our fortieth anniversary."

A general committee to oversee the effort was appointed, and a four-day campaign was planned. The plan devised by the committee called for 250 congregants to be organized into five regiments of ten companies each. Each regiment identified itself with one of the five colors in Martin Luther's shield: red, white, black, blue, and gold.

All told the effort involved 50 companies, each comprised of a team of five congregants. In four days, the 250 workers involved secured 1,308 pledges for a total gift of $45,901! This sum enabled the congregation to pay its mortgage in full as well as make repairs and improvements to the church. Making significant gifts at significant milestones in the life of Holy Trinity had become a tradition of this congregation, and would, undoubtedly, continue.

In 1920, a change was made that affects the congregation of Holy Trinity and its Church Council to this day. During that year, the annual meeting date for the Main Street parish was changed from May to January in order to correspond with planning done by the United Lutheran Church.

In May of 1921, a World War I memorial tablet given by the Men's Bible Class was unveiled. The following year, the surplus raised during the church's 40th anniversary was used to pay for maintenance and repairs on the 17 year-old building. Extensive repairs to the roofing were done as well as acoustical work on the church's ceiling. A position was added to the staff of Holy Trinity in 1922 as the church hired its first full-time secretary, Miss Lillian Stortz. In October of 1922, Holy Trinity's importance as the cathedral church of English Lutheranism continued to be solidified as it was the site for the important business sessions of the biennial convention of the United Lutheran Church.

Nineteen twenty - three was another active year in the life of Holy Trinity. The congregation contributed substantially to the building of a Lutheran church in Ithaca,

Part Two: The Kahler Years

New York, that would serve Cornell University and Ithaca College, as well as a new building for St. John's Orphan Home. During that same year, an important development in the future of Holy Trinity took place. A bequest of $1,000 was made to Holy Trinity in the will of Lambert Smith. This sum was set aside in order to begin an endowment fund. In the 90 years that have followed, the Holy Trinity Endowment Fund has been cultivated, developed and enhanced by the congregation.

In the fall of 1923, 32 year-old Henry J. Pflum, Jr., accepted the call to become associate pastor of Holy Trinity. On February 1, 1924 he resigned the pastorate of a Lutheran Church in Rockville Center, Long Island, to come to the Main Street church in Buffalo.

In October of 1924, Dr. and Mrs. Kahler celebrated their 40th year at Holy Trinity. Services of gratitude were held at the church as well as a congregational celebration of the anniversary. A gift of $3,000 was given to Dr. and Mrs. Kahler, and a portrait of Dr. Kahler by the widely recognized artist, Florence Bach, was commissioned. That portrait can still be seen in an area called The Gallery at Holy Trinity.

Heeding the advice of his family and his physician, 77 year-old Dr. Frederick A. Kahler retired from the ministry of Holy Trinity in June of 1927. He had been pastor of Holy Trinity for 44 years and had led the congregation during some its greatest growth and its biggest changes. The final decade of Dr. Kahler's ministry at Holy Trinity was one of much-deserved recognition and acclaim. It is no surprise that immediately after he retired, the congregation bestowed upon him the title of "Pastor Emeritus" at full salary. There was a provision with this title: that Dr. Kahler was to continue in the life and ministry of the church according to his own energy and desires.

The impact of Dr. Kahler on the life of the English Evangelical Lutheran Church of the Holy Trinity, the English Lutheran movement in Buffalo, and the many lives he touched was truly phenomenal. His biographer, Dr. Paul Bloomhardt, an assistant pastor at Holy Trinity from 1920-23, sums up his mentor best:

". . . . By unremitting toil and endless travel over the streets of the growing city he worked to draw an ever greater number of people into the fold of the church where he could care for them like a shepherd. They came from all classes of society and from many faiths . . . These, having experienced his strong helpfulness and warm-heartedness, brought others. . . . . Wherever he went he was the embodiment of a radiant optimism. He habitually influenced men and women to believe that the present, whether wholly satisfactory or not, was part of the road to better things. . . . "

During Holy Trinity's 125th anniversary year, the Rev. Dr. Charles Bang dedicated a sermon to the life and work of the one who served the longest tenure as pastor of Holy Trinity. Pastor Bang ended his sermon with these words:

"Today, 154 years after his birth, 73 years after his birthday into the kingdom, we say thanks be to God for all the saints, and thanks be to God for Frederick August Kahler."

Part Three: The Pflum Years

"O God our help in ages past,
our hope for years to come.
Our shelter from the stormy blast,
and our eternal home."

LBW Hymn 320

On June 26, 1927, the Reverend Henry J. Pflum, Jr., a native of Reading, Pennsylvania, was installed as pastor of Holy Trinity. As expressed in the 1979 history of the church, "Dr. Pflum had come to Buffalo in 1924, and now, three years later, found himself in the unenviable position of succeeding a legend." A reserved and introspective man, Dr. Pflum had already made an impact on the Lutheran community in Buffalo. In his second year at Holy Trinity, he started a Training School for Teachers comprised of Sunday School teachers from other congregations. He also began a Sunday School specifically for college students.

The first major event in Henry Pflum's pastorate at

Reverend Henry J. Pflum, the third pastor of Holy Trinity.

Holy Trinity occurred in 1929 when the church celebrated its 50th anniversary. As with previous milestones in the life of the congregation, a celebration was planned that included three services over a two-day period, eight guest pastors, special music by the choir, and a reception in the church's fellowship hall.

The celebration of Holy Trinity's 50th anniversary began at 10:45am on Sunday, May 5, 1929 with a procession to the hymn "Holy, Holy, Holy." The anniversary sermon was given at the first service by the Rev. Frank F. Fry, a high-ranking official of the United Lutheran Church.

The second service was held on Sunday evening, May 5. It featured greetings from two guest pastors, an address on Holy Trinity's history by Dr. Kahler, and remarks on the church's future by Pastor Pflum.

The third and final service of the 50th anniversary celebration was held on Tuesday, May 7, 1929. One newspaper account of this event termed it a "reunion service" as three of the four featured speakers that evening were former associate pastors at Holy Trinity. One of the three former associates, Dr. Paul Bloomhardt, said of the future of the church:

"Holy Trinity will, as of its first 50 years, meet the things that challenge during its next half century of life, with youthful resiliency."

As it had done previously, the congregation of Holy Trinity once again raised an anniversary gift that would be put into the Endowment Fund. The goal was set at $50,000 – a thousand dollars for each year in the history of the church. When all was said and done, the congregation again exceeded its goal as $52,049 was received.

In October of 1929, another 50th anniversary was celebrated at Holy Trinity. The opening paragraph of an article in *The Buffalo Courier* of October 25, 1929 describes it best:

". . . . Celebrating its 50th anniversary the Women's Society of Holy Trinity Lutheran Church gave a reception yesterday afternoon in the parish house at which the members recalled the fruitful years past and with rejoicing took an optimistic survey of the future. . . ."

Several speakers were featured at the reception, most notably, Mrs. Frederick Kahler, who gave a history of the Holy Trinity Women's Society. In her address, Mrs. Kahler described that the purpose of the Women's Society was to "foster friendliness, sociability in the congregation, to visit the sick and needy and to contribute to the needs of the church." Mrs. Kahler also highlighted a number of gifts the society had given to worthy benevolences. Among these was a donation to a theological seminary for the education of young ministers. The Holy Trinity Women's Society truly had much to celebrate that October afternoon. Its life as an organization of the church began with 14 charter members in 1879; in 1929, the Women's Society had grown to an active membership of 265.

In October of 1929, another event took place that would be felt across the United States: the crash of the stock market. The Great Depression would soon deepen across the country and it most certainly would be felt at

Holy Trinity. Still, Christian fellowship and good news continued at the Main Street church.

In June of 1930, Pastor Henry Pflum had conferred upon him the degree of Doctor of Divinity from Roanoke College. In October of the same year, the congregation continued its outreach by undertaking the support of an educational missionary at Andhra College in India.

By 1931, the Great Depression was being felt at Holy Trinity and, as the 1979 history of the church indicates, "Holy Trinity faced a situation new to this sturdy group; namely, numbers of its members were out of work." Amid these difficulties, in January of 1931, death came to 80 year-old Dr. Frederick A. Kahler, pastor emeritus of the church. *The Buffalo Courier* of January 27 announced: "Kahler Rites Tomorrow . . . . Clergyman's body to lie in state in Holy Trinity Church." *The Buffalo Evening News* of January 28 offered the following description of what took place in Holy Trinity's sanctuary before Dr. Kahler's funeral:

> *"For three hours before the services, long lines of people passed by the bier at which members of the church council stood guard. In the throng were many civic and church leaders of the city and from throughout the country."*

Dr. Kahler was eulogized by a number of dignitaries. *The Buffalo Evening News* reported that the service "was attended by an audience that crowded the church."

Amid the economic difficulties of the early 1930s and the loss of their beloved pastor emeritus, the congregation of Holy Trinity was resilient. Enthusiasm and activity continued to fill the Main Street church in Buffalo. A Men's

Part Three: The Pflum Years

Brotherhood was started to add to the excellent leadership exhibited by the church's women's groups. The Holy Trinity Sunday School continued to be strong. There was a call in the early 1930s for the church to employ a Director of Christian Education. This did not happen because of financial problems, but the idea remained and a seed was planted for the future.

Pageantry and theater took on a significant role at Holy Trinity in the 1930s. Photographs in the current archives of the church indicate that pageants of differing themes and for various occasions began to occur at Holy Trinity in the 1920s. By the early 1930s, the annual Christmas pageant became one of the biggest events of the church's calendar year. These "spectacles" involved many children, teenagers, choirs, and large numbers of volunteers. Staged with all the "theatrical trimmings," Christmas pageants at Holy Trinity involved beautiful costuming and set pieces – touches that would become traditions at the church for years to come. It should be noted that in December 1932, the Christmas Pageant at Holy Trinity was attended by 1,096 people. This incredible turnout necessitated the addition of a repeat performance on New Year's Eve. It was attended by an audience of 475.

The resilience of Holy Trinity in the early 1930s was born of a strong faith and the vision to continue the traditions of its ministry. Financial support for missionary work in India was continued inspite of financial difficulties. Within the church, the members of the congregation felt that music should continue to play an important role in Holy Trinity's mission and ministry. Music had always been significant at Holy Trinity and the church attempted to maintain this program. By 1930, the Holy Trinity choir, mainly a "volunteer" ensemble of parishioners, employed two paid soloists. For a period of two years, in the early 1930s, the soloists were discontinued for financial reasons. In 1934, Holy Trinity found a way to employ the two soloists again.

During the same year the soloists came back to Holy Trinity's choir, members of the congregation strengthened the social side of the church by forming a "Couple Club." This organization brought together young couples of the congregation. It became a strong program in the church, continuing for the next 40 years. The youth of Holy Trinity also continued to be active in the early to mid-1930s. By this period in time, the youth groups in the church became known as "Luther Leagues." Boy Scout and Girl Scout groups were also developed during the mid-1930s and quickly became active. They built a log cabin in the area of what is now the music studio of the church and used it for various scout training programs.

Dr. Henry Pflum faced a number of challenges during his 16-year pastorate at Holy Trinity. One of the most significant took place on Saturday, March 16, 1935. Around 11 o'clock that morning, an employee from a store near Holy Trinity noticed that the church was on fire. The store employee alerted the church sexton, James Wheaton, who, in turn, notified all in the church of the situation. At the time, Dr. Pflum was conducting a confirmation class of 16 girls and boys. The church secretary was on duty, and three church council members, including Council President Frederick Henrich, were having a meeting.

Upon being alerted that a fire was in progress, all those who were in the building evacuated the premises. According to a story in *The Buffalo Evening News* of March 16, 1935, the first alarm sounded at 11:20am. Not long after, the

Buffalo Fire Department arrived on the scene. According to Frederick Henrich, in his 1937 history of Holy Trinity, "Through the intelligent and well-directed efforts of the fire department, the building was saved and the loss kept at a minimum." It took firefighters a little more than an hour to put out the blaze. One fireman was overcome by smoke. He was revived at the scene and recovered.

Probably caused by a chimney spark, the fire was located in the attic space between the church ceiling in the nave and the roof of the building. The most serious damage caused in the event occurred in the attic space. The electric wiring that powered the lights in the cove (altar area) and the chandeliers in the sanctuary was completely destroyed. The damage to the rest of the building – mainly in the sanctuary – was due to water and smoke. Apparently firemen stationed themselves with fire hoses in the center aisle of the sanctuary in order to put out any other flames that appeared.

Dr. Ralph Loew, in his portion of the 1979 history, recounts that the fire at Holy Trinity caused quite a commotion:

". . . . Rumors spread through the city that the building was doomed, and hundreds of people, many members among them, were drawn to the scene, tying up traffic for blocks. . . ."

In the end, the church sustained a little over $10,000 in damages. The loss was covered by insurance. In their usual resilient manner, the congregation and its leaders had the roof of the church immediately repaired and the sanctuary made ready for Sunday worship. At the end of

Stand Fast Forever

The Buffalo Evening News account of this difficult day in the life of the church, Dr. Pflum was quoted as saying, "Services to be held in the church as usual tomorrow. . . ."

On April 13, 1935, a photograph of the Main Street church appeared in *The Buffalo Evening News.* The caption of the picture indicates that the congregation of Holy Trinity would observe the 30th anniversary of their current building on April 14, 1935. The damage from the fire of the previous month did not deter the faithful from celebrating another milestone in the life of their congregation.

By the mid-1930s, the Lutheran churches in Buffalo pooled their efforts in an attempt to deal with the unemployment situation in the city. Holy Trinity did its part as the "Committee on Relief" was created by the Church Council to assist those in the congregation who were needy. Meanwhile, Holy Trinity continued to look beyond its own walls for those it could help. The church answered special appeals from Canada and Russia, aided flood victims from Ohio, and, under the continued leadership of Frederick Henrich, raised $3,000 for the Cambridge Chapel. Dr. Ralph Loew, in the 1979 history of Holy Trinity, characterized the congregation at this time when he wrote:

> *"All of this benevolent work in a time of national depression is eloquent testimony to the steady and continuing leadership of the church and the faith of its members."*

In 1937, the first history of Holy Trinity was published. It was titled *A Short Biography of Frederick August Kahler, D.D., L.L.D. and An Historical Sketch of the Holy Trinity Church* and cost $1.25 in hard cover. Dr. Paul Bloomhardt, a former associate pastor of Holy Trinity, authored the biography of Dr. Kahler; Frederick Henrich, Church Council president, penned the brief history of the congregation.

As Holy Trinity celebrated its 60th anniversary in 1939 and moved its ministry into the 1940s, its tradition of having strong leaders within the congregation continued in a seamless fashion. The leadership of the congregation at its inception in 1879 bore names such as Hengerer, Becker, Kurtz, and Koons. By the turn of the 20th century, the mantle passed to parishioners named Ansteth, Smith, and Reeb. As Frederick Henrich's history of the congregation went to press, new leaders were emerging within the congregation. In the 1940s, new and lifelong members such as Edward Hoffman, Margarethe Kahler Henrich (daughter of Dr. Kahler) Dr. Kenneth Eckhert, Dr. George Eckhert, Dr. Mary Henrich Botsford (granddaughter of Dr. Kahler), and Dr. Walter Hoffman continued the traditions of Holy Trinity while moving the congregation in new directions.

In September 1943, Dr. Henry Pflum, Jr. resigned as pastor of Holy Trinity to accept a call to Christ Lutheran Church in Allentown, Pennsylvania. For the first time in 59 years, during the Second World War, the congregation had to search for a new pastor.

Part Four: The Loew Years

"Praise to the Lord, the Almighty,
the King of Creation.
O my soul, praise him,
for he is your health and salvation.
Let all who hear
Now to his temple draw near
Joining in glad adoration!"

LBW 543

Reverend Ralph W. Loew,
fourth pastor of
Holy Trinity, 1944

In the autumn of 1943, Holy Trinity found itself in an unusual and challenging position. The last time the church had gone through the process of selecting a pastor and extending a call to him was in 1884. Now, 59 years later, the Main Street cathedral of English Lutheranism would have to begin what would turn out to be a difficult and lengthy process to select its next spiritual leader.

The congregation of Holy Trinity went for eight frustrating months without a senior pastor. Finally, in

May of 1944, the answer the church had been hoping and praying for came when Holy Trinity was introduced to a native of Columbus, Ohio by the name of Ralph William Loew. At the time, Reverend Loew was 36 years old, husband of Maxine, father of a two year old daughter named Carolyn, and the associate pastor of The Lutheran Church of the Reformation in Washington, D. C. In a letter dated May 6, 1944 to Dr. Franklin C. Fry of Trinity Lutheran Church in Akron, Ohio, Dr. Loew expressed his feelings about a call to Western New York:

" . . . . It was good of you to write me with reference to the possibility of a call to Holy Trinity at Buffalo. I think you know what a happy situation this has been at Reformation. Pulling up the roots from here isn't easy.

Nonetheless, there's a compelling challenge about the work and its possibilities at Buffalo. I'm going to be visiting there again during the coming week and we shall probably settle the matter at that time . . . ."

About a week later, Ralph Loew was a guest preacher at Sunday morning services at Holy Trinity. After church, he was extended a unanimous call by the congregation to become its fourth pastor in 65 years. According to a story in *The Buffalo Evening News* of May 15, 1944, Dr. Loew indicated he would accept the call to Holy Trinity "pending approval by The Church of the Reformation, Washington."

Pastor Ralph Loew came to Holy Trinity at a very challenging time in the life of the Main Street congregation. The effects of the Second World War were being felt within the church. As Mrs. Kenneth Eckhert, Sr. recalled in her portion of the 1979 history of Holy Trinity:

"Widespread employment of men and women in defense industries was eroding church attendance and, together with gasoline rationing, made it difficult for families to bring their children to Sunday School."

Mrs. Eckhert adds that buses had to be chartered to transport children to church from several districts in the city of Buffalo.

The strongest effect of World War II on Holy Trinity was that 150 members of the church were drawn into military service; seven ultimately died in battle. Yet, amid all the turmoil, the congregation was optimistic; they sensed that in Ralph Loew they had called a man who would lead Holy Trinity into a new era of growth and continue to build the church's prominence in the city of Buffalo.

At the end of the summer of 1945, the United States celebrated "Victory in Japan." Church services were held all over the country and many gave thanks for the end of the Second World War. After a number of services of thanksgiving at Holy Trinity, a group of five churchmen, moved by a sermon given by Pastor Loew, cabled $1200 to a Lutheran pastor in Germany named Martin Niemöller. In a note accompanying the gift, they wrote, "Use this to bring hope." Two years later, they would find out how powerful their gift had been.

The same lay leaders, after committing their gift to the Lutheran pastor, sent $1200 to the United Lutheran Church's Board of Foreign Missions in order to support a missionary in Japan. Finally, these churchmen made a commitment to a budgetary formula to devote equal amounts of funding to benevolent causes and to the programs within the church. In a spirit seen along many turns in Holy Trinity's road, the strengthening of faith within the walls of the church once again was achieved by reaching out with projects that touched many lives beyond the sanctuary on Main Street.

In 1946, Holy Trinity purchased property that was located in its "backyard" at 33 and 37 Linwood Avenue. This would allow for the development of a parking area. With a vision for the future, the acquisition of this property would become even more important twenty years later. Also during 1946, an exchange of property gave the congregation access to both the north and south sides of the church. Now, the Holy Trinity Church "campus" was protected and moved members of the church to begin pondering the possibility of a chapel.

It should be pointed out that the social side of Holy Trinity also continued to develop in 1946. During that year, Maxine Loew, wife of the pastor, created a "Mother's Class." It would become the "Mother's Club" and, eventually, would evolve into a group known as "Mothers and Others."

In 1947, Holy Trinity continued to extend its ministry across the globe. During that year, the congregation learned that 7,500 East German refugees had relocated in Heilsberg, West Germany, but had no place to worship. In response, the congregation gave $10,000 to be used for the building of a church. In February 1947, a memorable event in the life of the congregation took place when Holy Trinity was visited by Rev. Martin Niemöller. During the February 23 worship service, Pastor Niemöller expressed his gratitude for the gift of $1200 that had been sent by the church in August 1945. The congregation learned that morning that Pastor Niemöller received their gift soon after his release from a Nazi concentration camp where he had been confined for eight years. The congregants also learned that the gift they sent had been used to feed starving people in Berlin.

Nineteen forty-seven was significant in the life of Pastor Loew. During that busy year, he was chosen as an official delegate to the organizing convention of the Lutheran World Federation in Sweden, and was awarded the degree of Doctor of Divinity by Wittenberg University in his native Ohio.

Finally, in this period of time, it was decided that maintaining and improving the church structure was vital to the future of the congregation. With that in mind, the Greater Holy Trinity Fund was begun in order to increase the value and usefulness of the almost fifty-year-old building. One other "internal" development took place at Holy Trinity in 1947 that had great ramifications with regard to the church's strong and highly-valued music program. The Church Council created the full-time position of Director of Music. It would be this person's mission to create an all-encompassing ministry of music within the church. Not only would this musician play the organ during worship services, he or she would be responsible for developing and leading a series of church choirs. The first Director of Music hired for this demanding task was a nationally known organist, choir director, and composer by the name of Dr. Roberta Bitgood.

A gift was given to Holy Trinity in 1948 that still touches the congregation today. That year, Dr. and Mrs. William H. Mansperger, among the well-known lay leaders of Holy Trinity, gave the church a set of magnificent stained glass chancel windows which replaced the original Tiffany-style windows. A description of the stained glass windows from the 1979 history of the church captures them best:

". . . . The five slender lancets are each twenty feet in height and contain thousands of pieces of imported glass.

They depict the great central purpose of the church as they spread before the worshipper a vast panorama of rich color and lift the eyes to the sweeping lines of the vaulted ceiling. . . . "

Henry Lee Willett, a distinguished craftsman in stained glass, designed the windows. Suggestions for the scenes depicted came from Dr. Loew. The 1979 history vividly describes some of what can be seen in the striking artwork in the stained glass:

"Symbolic scenes . . . range from the reaping of grain by a farmer and the rearing of a child by its mother to the creating of the world by God and the gathering of all races and peoples into the universal church. Characters run the gamut from Moses to representatives of modern arts and sciences . . ."

Dr. William Mansperger, whose generous gift to Holy Trinity led to the building of the church's chapel.

The contributions to Holy Trinity by Dr. and Mrs. Mansperger can still be seen and appreciated today. Dr. Mansperger began practicing medicine in the late 1890s. According to the 1979 history of Holy Trinity, he brought many medical firsts to Buffalo. The first infant incubator, the first thyroid operation, and the first spinal anesthesia are among the innovations developed by

Dr. Mansperger. He and his wife so loved Holy Trinity that they made possible many innovations in and around the church.

The year after the installation of the stained glass windows, more new additions were made in the sanctuary. In 1949, Mrs. Frederick Henrich and Miss Olive Breitweiser gave Holy Trinity a baptismal transept. The pictorial window, "Christ Blessing The Children," which had originally been placed in the middle of the south wall, was relocated to the new transept in order to provide a companion symbol to the meaning of baptism. It should be noted that Holy Trinity's bronze angel baptismal font has been moved around the sanctuary a number of times – from the front to the back and from one side to the other. (It has been in its present location since the most recent renovation of the sanctuary in the mid 1990s.)

Amid all the changes in the building Holy Trinity celebrated its 70th anniversary. In honor of this milestone, the congregation created a special fund of $35,000 to help finance improvements to the church.

Finally, in 1949, a major addition to the parish's music program crowned what must have been an exciting year in the life of the church. Thanks to a generous bequest, on May 1 of this 70th anniversary year, a new four manual Möller pipe organ was dedicated. This instrument had 44 ranks of pipes and was the first new postwar organ installed in a downtown church in Buffalo. It was soon recognized as being one of the city's finest.

As Holy Trinity entered the 1950s, it continued to serve a vital role in the city of Buffalo. In 1950, the church established a permanent year-round Evangelism Committee. In 1951, the congregation contributed both

Part Four: The Loew Years

leadership and resources toward the building of an addition to the Lutheran Church Home for the Aged. Dr. Kenneth Eckhert, a dedicated member of Holy Trinity, served as general chairman of an interchurch fund drive to raise $250,000 for the project. Holy Trinity gave $54,000 toward the addition. Miss Margaret L. Wendt, who co-directed the fund-raising effort at Holy Trinity, made a personal contribution that included the dining room in the new wing of the Lutheran Home.

The following year, in the spirit of benevolence so characteristic of the cathedral church of English Lutheranism in Buffalo, the Sunday School children of Holy Trinity sent a donation to India to help rebuild a high school that was destroyed in a storm. During that same year, as the church once more was reaching beyond its own walls to fulfill a need across the world, it opened its own doors to a group of Estonians looking for a place to worship. Residents of the tiny nation of Estonia, these Lutherans had fled their homeland before it was invaded by communist armies. The Estonian congregation called Pastor Elmar Pahn to be their minister — a capacity in which he served for nine years. It should be mentioned that the Estonians still make Holy Trinity their place of worship using the chapel of the Main Street church for their services.

In terms of milestones in the history of Holy Trinity, the church's 75th anniversary was both proud and powerful. In 1954, the congregation could feel a strong sense of accomplishment. In the ten years that Dr. Loew had been pastor, the interior of the church had been beautifully and purposefully enhanced. In that same period of time, the congregation had reached far beyond its own walls to profoundly touch lives in Europe and Asia with its assistance. Finally, Holy Trinity could see the impact of its support locally in the Lutheran Home for the Aged. Reflecting on all the church had accomplished in 75 years, the congregation had much to celebrate.

Powerful events of 1954 would have a profound effect on the future of Holy Trinity. For this particular anniversary of the church, the congregation pledged $75,000 in celebration of dedicated Christian fellowship and service in the city of Buffalo. The fund would enable Holy Trinity to carry out special projects within the church, guarantee the congregation's future, and provide for a $20,000 gift for the New Niagara Lutheran Home for Invalid Aged. Once again, another milestone in the church's history was characterized by congregational giving, a vision for the work that was needed, both in and beyond the sanctuary, and a bright, faith-filled view of the church's future. To commemorate a rich past and a promising future, members of the congregation wrote and staged an anniversary pageant that played to a crowded church.

In the Diamond Jubilee year of Holy Trinity, several new faces came into the Main Street church who would become important in the life of the congregation. It was during this particular year that Otto and Lilly Rosin began their long relationship with Holy Trinity as caretakers of the church. John Becker became Holy Trinity's director of music. Also, in 1954, Holy Trinity welcomed a new assistant pastor. As the congregation celebrated its 75th anniversary, it began what would be an important association with the recently ordained Rev. Matthew Littleton Winters.

Finally, amid all the activity in the church during 1954, the seeds of what had been a dream were given the chance to grow into reality. After the death of his wife, Dr.

William Mansperger approached Dr. Loew about building a chapel for Holy Trinity in her memory. Six years earlier, Dr. Mansperger and his wife had given five stained glass windows for the chancel in the sanctuary. Now, continuing to show his great faith in Holy Trinity's mission, this influential member of the congregation wanted to create what had been dreamt about for some time. Eight weeks after Dr. Mansperger offered his gift to Holy Trinity, he died suddenly. At this time, there had been a plan developed to turn a room in the church into the new chapel. With Dr. Mansperger's passing, this idea came to a stop – temporarily. A generous bequest in the physician's will, including his Jewett Parkway home, would have profound effects on the congregation's future. Holy Trinity was able to acquire property immediately adjacent to the church, demolish an unsightly building, and create the space to construct a chapel. This bequest, in time, would also allow for the construction of Trinity Tower.

The year after Holy Trinity joyously celebrated its Diamond Jubilee, the church mourned the loss of one of its true pioneers. In 1955, Frederick Henrich died at the age of eighty-six. Mrs. Kenneth Eckhert, Sr., in her portion of the 1979 history of Holy Trinity described Frederick Henrich as a "lifelong leader, worker, and Christian gentleman." Mrs. Eckhert added, "In a sense his passing marked the end of an era, for he was the last member of that sturdy group whose consecrated thinking and wise direction had given the excellent start to the story of this congregation." Frederick Henrich's 1937 writing of that story would prove to be an important legacy of his for years to come.

By 1955, Dr. Loew's abilities as a preacher and scholar were attracting national attention. During this year, he embarked on an important lecture tour for the United Lutheran Church in America. Nineteen fifty-five was also a strong year for Holy Trinity's music program. It was during this time that the annual Three Choir Hymn Festival was started. This event united the choirs of Holy Trinity, St. Paul's Episcopal Cathedral, and Westminster Presbyterian Church. The following year, the Lutheran Chorale was developed. Represented in this ensemble were members of many of the Lutheran churches in Western New York. Once again, the Main Street church held high the banner of this musical endeavor as the Chorale was under the direction of Holy Trinity's John Becker.

In April 1957, the national spotlight was again on Dr. Loew as *Life Magazine* published his sermon, "The Eternity of a Little While," calling it one of America's six most notable Easter messages. Along with Dr. Loew's writing was a picture of him taken in the church by world-renowned photographer Alfred Eisenstadt. Toward the end of 1957, Holy Trinity marked yet another beginning. On November 3 of that year, ground breaking ceremonies for the Mansperger Chapel took place. With plans for an addition to the church campus developed by architects Shelgren and Whitman, construction was ready to begin. Once again, with great faith and a vision for Holy Trinity's future, the congregation, led by Building Committee Chairman Dr. Kenneth Eckhert, embarked on a project that they knew was needed. Work on the new chapel complex went on throughout 1958; the building was completed early the following year.

Services of dedication of the new chapel were held on January 25, 1959. On the front cover of the bulletin for this event, the Mansperger Chapel was dedicated:

"To the Glory of God."

"To the Continuing Ministry of Word and Sacraments."

"To the Faith in the Essential Place of this Church at the Heart of the Niagara Frontier."

With the completion of the Mansperger Chapel complex, it would now be possible to have a place of worship for Matins and Vesper Services, weekly children's services, a place for seminars and study groups, a meeting place for organizations in the church, a cultural center for programs of music and art, and much more.

Originally, the design of the chapel was to be in Tudor Gothic. In the end, due to financial considerations and the desire to express, as the dedication bulletin indicates, "the quality of Christian faith in dynamic terms," the architects and the Building Committee were to opt for a contemporary design.

The six windows in the chapel were, and still are, one of the most striking characteristics of the building. Following along the east side of the chapel, the Prayer Window, the Children's Window, the Marriage Window, the Community Window, the Resurrection Window, and the Healing Window each convey a unique Christian message to the viewer. Like the stained glass chancel windows in the main sanctuary, these were designed by Henry Lee Willett from suggestions given by Dr. Loew.

The chapel was equipped with a specially designed organ. This instrument had 12 ranks of pipes and would serve the church well until it was removed during the 125th anniversary of Holy Trinity 45 years later, in 2004.

The chapel complex at Holy Trinity was constructed with a meditation room, a chapel narthex, the Fellowship Room, a kitchen, a bride's room, and two restrooms. Fifty years later, this facility continues to be a valuable and purposeful part of the Holy Trinity Church campus. A verse in the chapel dedication bulletin of January 25, 1959 sums it up best:

"Here may Thy children meet in glad devotion:
Here may Thy Way be taught:
Here may Thy Name be hallowed:
Here may Thy praises be sung:

Here may life in its fullness be nourished and guided:
Here may the bonds of fellowship
be strengthened in loving service."

It should be noted that another event took place at Holy Trinity on January 25, 1959: the relighting of the main sanctuary. When the 75th Anniversary Fund was raised in 1954, one of the projects planned was to install new lighting in the church "auditorium." Holy Trinity brought in the nationally known lighting consultant Svend Brukun, and based on his recommendations, changes were made. The original bronze chandeliers were removed, and ten gothic lanterns, still in the sanctuary today, were hung from the trefoils of the clerestory windows. Additionally, recessed lights were placed throughout the nave. All of the new lighting was first used the same day the chapel was dedicated.

All of these new developments made for quite a celebration of the church's 80th anniversary. The congregation

Holy Trinity Lutheran Church in the early 1950's

could look upon its "church campus" with pride and the realization that a tradition begun by the founders of Holy Trinity was kept strong and alive. A pattern had emerged at Holy Trinity through 80 years of existence: greet each milestone not only with celebration but with strong faith in action. In 1959, Dr. Ralph Loew could look back over the first fifteen years of his pastorate and know that the theme of Holy Trinity under his leadership – pursuing projects to strengthen God's kingdom – continued to build momentum.

One other project of note was begun during the 80th anniversary year: with funds from the sale of Dr. Mansperger's home, Holy Trinity purchased a lot on Depew Avenue in Buffalo with the intent to build a parsonage.

The English Evangelical Lutheran Church of the Holy Trinity reached its 81st year in 1960. During that year,

John F. Kennedy, after a contentious race against Richard M. Nixon, was elected President of the United States. Rock 'n' roll music had become a popular and permanent facet of American culture. Television was firmly implanted in homes across the country and becoming a powerful communication force in American life. The United States was turning its eyes toward the heavens in a race with the Soviet Union to put a human being in outer space. Change was in the air, and change came to Holy Trinity.

During 1960, construction was begun on the church's parsonage on Depew Avenue. An additional gift to Holy Trinity by another of its faithful benefactors, Dr. George Haller, made this project possible. Also in the same year, Pastor Matthew L. Winters accepted a call to the pastorate of Trinity Lutheran Church in Camp Hill, Pennsylvania. Fifteen years later, the road in Pastor Winter's faith journey would lead him back to Holy Trinity – to become Dr. Loew's successor! Finally, 1960 saw Holy Trinity begin a new venture in the arts with the creation of the Trinity Players — a theater group within the church dedicated to staging religious drama. Their inaugural production was Thornton Wilder's "Our Town."

For many years, Holy Trinity had been a member of the United Lutheran Church in America. In 1962, after a merger of several Lutheran church organizations in the U.S., Holy Trinity became a member of the new "Lutheran Church in America" (LCA). Dating back to Dr. Kahler's administration, leaders from the Main Street church had been called to and involved with their denomination on a national level. Once again, Holy Trinity would be represented nationally on councils organized to move the new body of Lutheran churches forward. Dr. Loew was

Part Four: The Loew Years

made a member of the LCA's Executive Board and Dr. Kenneth Eckhert was elected to the organization's new Board of Theological Education. In the summer of 1963, Dr. Loew was an official delegate to the Fourth Assembly of the Lutheran World Federation at Helsinki, Finland. At this gathering, over 700 delegates were present representing 72 million Lutherans around the world. As Holy Trinity approached its 85th anniversary, the church could be proud as its stature locally, nationally, and internationally continued to grow. Then, a powerful moment in the church's history began on March 8, 1964.

After the usual Sunday morning worship services that day, an official meeting of the congregation was held in which all present heard an announcement that, at that time, had to be shocking: Dr. Ralph W. Loew was requesting that he be able to resign his pastorate at Holy Trinity. Dr. Loew wanted to leave the Main Street cathedral of English Lutheranism to accept a call to become Pastor of the new Christ the King Church in Chicago, Illinois. According to Mrs. Kenneth Eckhert, in the 1979 history of the church, "Dr. Loew's announcement of his resignation stunned not only members of Holy Trinity, but the entire community."

Six weeks later, upon assessing all the problems with the "Chicago project," Dr. Loew asked for the withdrawal of his resignation. At the conclusion of the worship service on Sunday, April 26, 1964, a reconsideration of Dr. Loew's resignation was announced to the congregation. One week later, a joint resolution of the Church Council and the Pulpit Committee was submitted to the congregation requesting that Dr. Loew continue his ministry at Holy Trinity. The joint resolution was unanimously accepted.

In the *Our Church Paper* issue of June 1964, Dr. Loew

published a statement in which he warmly characterized the church leadership in what was a time of tension and turmoil:

"Through these weeks, Mrs. Loew and I have been conscious more than ever of the loyalty, the wise counsel, and the friendship of the leaders of this church.... The members of the Executive and Pulpit Committee, the members of the Church Council and various leaders of the congregation have been of sustaining strength and remarkable friendship.

We have always known that, but it has been emphasized in these weeks ... "

The reaction of the congregation to the continuance of Ralph Loew's ministry at Holy Trinity was not only one of joy, but of a new need for faith in action. Milton Praker, president of the Church Council in 1964, published a statement in the same June issue of *Our Church Paper* in which he wrote:

".... This is a time for a reappraisal of Holy Trinity's place and purpose in downtown Buffalo, for a renewal of our faith, and for a reactivation of our energies and imagination.... Let each of us resolve to start the next era with renewed devotion...."

During the same month Dr. Loew was requested to continue as Holy Trinity's pastor, the church recognized its 85th anniversary. This celebration was filled with much joy and gratitude. There was also, no doubt, a renewed and strengthened closeness between the congregation and their pastor.

Reverend Ralph Loew at left and Holy Trinity congregation President, Milton Praker, right, at the presentation of a painting of Dr. Loew in the early 1960's. The identity of the man at the far left is unknown.

In 1966, another memorial gift to the church led to another proud dedication. The Edward Henrich family gave Holy Trinity a magnificent bell tower. The structure, made of self-weathering Mayari steel, was placed at the entrance of the Mansperger Chapel where it still stands today. The five bronze bells in the tower are pitched like those of St. Stephen's Cathedral in Vienna – the place where the Hapsburg kaisers of Austria and later, the emperors of the Austro-Hungarian Empire, were crowned.

The mid to late 1960s was a turbulent period in American history. Signs of a society in turmoil could be seen across the country. Demonstrations were taking place on college campuses, and city streets were the scenes of riots and violence. American culture was changing. A "generation gap" had developed, the civil rights movement was gaining momentum, an equal rights movement was emerging, concepts of morality were changing, and a resistance to structured forms of religion was taking hold. Amid all of this, Holy Trinity stayed true to its mission and took action in the face of a difficult time in Buffalo.

In order to strengthen the city in a time of uncertainty, Holy Trinity provided both leadership and resources. In 1967, Holy Trinity chose to be the host of a "Head Start" school financed by the federal poverty program. As explained by Mrs. Kenneth Eckhert in the 1979 history of the church, "This experiment sought to prepare disadvantaged children for education in public schools by imparting some of the fundamental skills which more fortunate youngsters learn at home."

Dr. Loew's leadership in the civic affairs of Buffalo continued to grow in this era. He had already communicated his humanitarian message through radio, television, and newspaper columns. In 1967, Dr. Loew was elected president of the Community Action Organization of Buffalo and Erie County. He would be called upon again – a year later – to lead more community renewal endeavors.

Finally, at a time when ecumenicalism was evolving in the Western New York community, Holy Trinity collaborated with the Roman Catholic Diocese of Buffalo to establish the Haller Interfaith Student Center in 1967. Created for those who attended nearby business schools, it was housed in a former private residence north of the church. The purpose of the center was to bring students and faculty together in an open and informal atmosphere. In this place, individuals of different backgrounds and beliefs could communicate

Part Four: The Loew Years

and gain a greater faith in their own religious convictions. Once again, a gift made this project possible as Dr. George Haller gave the private residence to Holy Trinity.

In 1968, Dr. Loew was called on again by the Buffalo community. This time, he headed "Project Good Neighbor" which was an effort mounted to strengthen open housing laws in the city. The Lutheran community in Buffalo came together in March of 1968 with a project to encourage new work and witness in a difficult time. Holy Trinity and seven other congregations, after many meetings, formed the "Lutheran Coordinated Ministry." Once again, with Holy Trinity at the core of the effort, the Lutheran churches of Buffalo collaborated not only to spread the good news of Christ, but also to improve their city.

In 1969, Holy Trinity reached another milestone – its 90th anniversary – with much ceremony and joy. On May 4 of that year, Holy Trinity celebrated "nine remarkable decades" with an event called "Lutheran Church Night." The evening began with a program of music by the Brass Wind Ensemble from the State University of New York at Buffalo. Following the pealing of the tower bells at 8 p.m., the congregation and choir engaged in singing four great hymns of the church beginning with "O God, Our Help In Ages Past" and concluding with "A Mighty Fortress is our God." The address for this milestone in the history of Holy Trinity was given by Dr. Robert J. Marshall, the newly-chosen president of the Lutheran Church in America. In his sermon that evening, Dr. Marshall challenged the Lutheran community to translate the heritage of the past into a continuing, innovative, and creative ministry for the present. After the sermon, all in the congregation joined in an act of rededication to the call that first formed the church. Mrs. Kenneth Eckhert, in the 1979 history, recalls how the evening ended:

"The whole event was one of excitement and celebration, highlighted by the spontaneous standing ovation and applause coming at the close of the postlude."

It certainly was a night to remember as well as a time to look forward, with much faith, to Holy Trinity's future.

Holy Trinity reached its 91st year in 1970. Richard M. Nixon was President of the United States. The much debated Vietnam War, often igniting protests, was still being fought. "Hippies" were now a part of the American scene and most evident on college campuses. Many social changes were sweeping across the country. Amid it all, Holy Trinity continued on a path of creation and imagination. Twenty-four years earlier, in 1946, the Church had purchased the lot at 33 Linwood Avenue – the site of the old Coit mansion. The property had originally been secured both for a parking area and for the future development of the church. In time, future development was uppermost in the minds of the leaders of Holy Trinity as they saw that the Linwood site would be an ideal location for an apartment complex for the elderly. Discussions were commenced with the New York State Division of Housing and Community Renewal. This agency agreed heartily with the idea. Conferences and planning sessions then took place which met with problems, difficulties and discouragement. Finally, in 1970, permission was granted for the Linwood House Association to begin construction.

After years of planning and anticipation, actual construction of the apartment for the aged — named "Trinity Tower" — was begun on October 7, 1970. Work

Part Four: The Loew Years

on the structure would proceed rapidly.

In 1971, as the girders of Trinity Tower were going up behind the church, Holy Trinity both received a gift and took on yet another project. The gift was a handsome Baldwin grand piano for the music studio presented by Dorothy and Virginia Mayer in memory of their parents. The Mayer family had been a part of the congregation for generations, and the Mayer sisters were considered among the most loyal members of the Chancel Choir.

The 1971 project that Holy Trinity undertook began with a request from Rev. Richard L. Peterman, director of special gifts for the Lutheran Church in America. He asked the Main Street church to give financial aid for basic medical care for 5,000 people on John's Island, South Carolina. The congregation of Holy Trinity responded with a $20,000 gift which became seed money for additional funds from two federal agencies. All of these funds made it possible to start a medical center on the island.

Finally, after thirteen months of construction, Trinity Tower was dedicated on December 10, 1971. The special guest in attendance at this event was the Hon. George W. Romney, U.S. Secretary of Housing and Urban Development. Secretary Romney cut the ribbon, and in his address, commended Holy Trinity for its faith in sponsoring the apartment building. In the 1979 history of the church, an interesting fact about the eight-story building is mentioned:

". . . . It is worth noting that Trinity Tower represented the first private development in Buffalo in which financing through the New York State Housing and Urban Renewal Commission was combined with federal subsidy loans."

Holy Trinity was back in the national spotlight in 1971 when *The Lutheran* magazine published a feature article about the church in its April 7 issue. Written by Carl F. Vehling the story characterized Holy Trinity as a community-minded parish with a progressive, active congregation. The article also profiled Dr. Ralph Loew and described him as "a reconciler, finding the good in everybody and bringing the pieces back together."

In 1972, John Becker left Holy Trinity closing his distinguished tenure as director of music. For eighteen years he had provided leadership for the church in music, worship and the arts – areas always important in the life of Holy Trinity Church. Mr. Becker was replaced by Frank Novak who continued the church's tradition of excellent music by starting a new series of concerts known as "Holy Trinity Sundays at Five."

Nineteen seventy-four was another milestone year for Holy Trinity as the Main Street church celebrated its 95th anniversary. As usual, to mark the occasion, the congregation undertook yet another project – this time, an internal one. A major renovation of the church offices was completed under the leadership of Clifford Hehr, chairman of the Renovation Committee. Mr. Hehr designed functional improvements and supervised structural changes and the installation of contemporary furnishings in this part of the church. The new church office complex was designated "The Haller Memorial Administrative Center" as the renovation was made possible by a gift from the Haller estate.

The 95th anniversary celebration at Holy Trinity was marked also by a homecoming. Skylab astronaut Dr. Edward Gibson, who had been an acolyte and confirmand at Holy Trinity, presented an illustrated tour of his 84-day

Dr. Loew looks on as Skylab Astronaut, Dr. Edward Gibson shakes hands with Matthew Bauer, brother of the author of this book in 1974. The girl at the right is unknown.

Skylab experience. Over 700 attended the event and greeted Dr. Gibson in the parish hall following his presentation. It should be noted that the author of this history and his family attended this event making their first visit to Holy Trinity. Eight years later, they would become members of the church.

Keeping with tradition, Holy Trinity had its "95th Anniversary Festival Service" on May 5, 1974. Music accented the event as the church organ was joined by trumpets, trombones, and tympani. Featured in the service were two traditional hymns arranged by Czech composer

Vaclav Nelhybel. "Built on a Rock," the processional hymn, was played to a setting commissioned especially for the 95th Anniversary Service. Dr. Loew wrote a special lyric that served as the final stanza of the hymn:

"More than the years relate the theme
Of faith and fellowship growing.
More than tradition and the scheme
Of hallowed customs approving,
Lord, move with newness through this church
Grant it bold courage and rebirth
Rejoicing in its high calling."

Following the festival service a commemorative program celebrating the 95th anniversary of the church took place after which a special meal was served by the Estonian congregation of Holy Trinity.

Finally, in 1974, Dr. Loew was named Director of Religion at the Chautauqua Institution. That same year, after 30 years at the Main Street church, the pastor who came to Holy Trinity at the age of thirty-six and the height of the Second World War announced his retirement. Ralph William Loew was sixty-six years old and could look back over a distinguished career of extraordinary leadership and active Christian witness while being committed to his true calling: serving as a parish pastor. As Mrs. Kenneth Eckhert states in the 1979 history of Holy Trinity, the impact of Dr. Loew's ministry was testimony to a "faith tremendous." "Under his leadership," she wrote, "Holy Trinity achieved prominence not only in Buffalo, but across the land. Because of his ministry, Holy Trinity became known throughout the world as a caring, sharing, proclaiming center of Christian witness.

Part Four: The Loew Years

A photograph of Reverend Ralph Loew taken near the time of his retirement.

When other churches sought to develop an increased program of mission and ministry, Holy Trinity was among the models to which they turned. It is impossible to fully measure the contributions of Dr. and Mrs. Loew to the life of this congregation."

The congregation held a retirement dinner for Dr. and Mrs. Loew shortly before his "official" retirement date of May 1, 1975. More than 725 persons gathered in the Golden Ballroom of the Statler Hilton Hotel in downtown Buffalo to pay tribute to a man whose ministry had touched many lives in 31 years. The booklet published for Holy Trinity's 95th anniversary characterized Dr. Loew's pastorate as "a ministry of concern – concern for the community, concern for his church, and especially concern for the individual. It has been this concern for people that has kept Holy Trinity healthy and growing in faith in a time when throughout the world the Church is being doubted, questioned, and downgraded."

In a local newspaper story titled "725 Bid Farewell as Dr. R. W. Loew Prepares to Leave Holy Trinity Parish," reporter Tom James describes the tribute to Dr. Loew, by the congregation, as "a prolonged standing ovation." Dr. Loew later said to all in attendance, "We have had our share of successes and defeats, and many times came close to falling on our face, but you had faith and believed in us. I am grateful tonight when we shift gears and go into a new venture, you still have faith in us." Such was the relationship shared by the congregation of Holy Trinity and their parish pastor from Columbus, Ohio.

As Dr. and Mrs. Loew began a new phase of their lives, Holy Trinity was now confronted with the kind of project it hadn't engaged in since 1944: calling a new pastor to serve in its pulpit. To fill the void, the Church Council, led by President Layton Leiser, would take their search to Camp Hill, Pennsylvania.

Part Five: The Winters Years
1975-1992

"No strength of ours can match his might!
We would be lost, rejected.
But now a champion comes to fight
Whom God himself elected."

LBW 229

Martin Luther

The year was 1975. Gerald Ford was in his first full year as President of the U.S. and was trying to heal the nation from the pain caused by the Watergate scandal. The Vietnam War finally came to an end. The late night television program "Saturday Night Live" debuted which continued to move youth culture to the forefront of American society.

Reverend Matthew L. Winters III, the fifth pastor of Holy Trinity, 1975

In the spring of 1975, with the retirement of Dr. Loew, Holy Trinity now had to deal with a circumstance it hadn't faced since 1944: the

need to find a new senior pastor. On the front cover of the April 1975 issue of "Our Church Paper" – which paid tribute to Ralph Loew – a brief article was published with the headline, "Call Extended to Pastor Winters." The story read as follows:

"On Sunday, March 16, 1975, a special congregational meeting was held in the sanctuary of the church, presided over by Dr. Edward K. Perry, President of the Upper New York Synod. Mr. Layton Leiser, President of the Church Council of Holy Trinity, read a resolution from the Church Council recommending that a call be extended to the Rev. Matthew L. Winters to become Senior Pastor of Holy Trinity Lutheran Church. The congregation approved the resolution and an official call has been issued to Pastor Winters and we are awaiting his formal acceptance. We pray God's blessings and guidance as these important decisions are made concerning the future of Holy Trinity."

The May 1975 issue of *Our Church Paper* then trumpeted wonderful news to the congregation: "Meet Our New Pastor: The Rev. Matthew L. Winters, D.D." In a letter to Church Council President Layton Leiser published in the same issue, Pastor Winters wrote,

"It is with humbleness and gratitude that I accept the call of Holy Trinity Lutheran Church to become Senior Pastor, as of August 1, 1975. To the best of my ability, I will be a faithful minister of the word and sacraments, and I will labor with you to maintain the wonderful tradition that is Holy Trinity's."

Pastor Winters went on in his letter to look upon his call "back" to Holy Trinity as "a wonderful opportunity." He finished his acceptance with these words:

"I believe the Lord has prepared me for this moment and I am eager to serve Him in your midst. I ask of you – your prayers – as we prepare for this next chapter in Holy Trinity's history."

Dr. Loew wrote a column in the May 1975 "Our Church Paper" where he made a few suggestions "on greeting a new pastor." One of these is entitled "We All Have a New Chapter." Dr. Loew wrote:

"The past has been exciting, especially at Holy Trinity Church. Yet, let us not cloud up a new day by too frequently reporting, 'You know, we used to do it this way.' There are new insights and new expressions required for this new chapter."

Pastor Winters, wife Elizabeth and daughter Deborah.

The Rev. Dr. Matthew Littleton Winters III, a graduate of Wittenberg University and the Hamma Divinity School, became senior pastor of Holy Trinity on August 1, 1975 at the age of 49. He left Buffalo and Holy Trinity in 1960 to accept an opportunity to become senior pastor of Trinity Lutheran Church in Camp Hill, Pennsylvania. Now, fifteen years later, he was "coming home" with his wife, Elizabeth, and children, Deborah and Matthew IV, to begin the next chapter in his ministry and the life of Holy Trinity Church.

As the 1979 history of the church indicates, the congregation was delighted to welcome back the Winters family and was surprised to see how the children, Deborah and Matt, had changed. "Young Matt" was now taller than his father and by this time had found a passion for baseball. It would indeed be a proud moment for Holy Trinity when, several years later, the New York Yankees made the pastor's son, then a senior at Williamsville South High School, their number one draft choice.

Not long after Pastor Winters returned to Holy Trinity, the church was presented with an opportunity to take on another project. In 1976, the Lutheran World Federation made an urgent appeal to the Main Street church. Holy Trinity responded by sponsoring a family of six Laotian refugees. Church members immediately assisted in finding them housing and employment, and the entire family eventually became baptized Christians.

An unusual event also took place at Holy Trinity in 1976. For only the second time in the church's 97-year history, a sermon was delivered in German. This address took place on Reformation Day and was given by Assistant Pastor Joachim K. Wilck.

In 1977, the year of the great blizzard in Western New York, Dr. Loew was elected "Pastor Emeritus" by the congregation of Holy Trinity. The last time this happened was in the year 1927 when Pastor Kahler was given the "Emeritus" title. During the same year that Dr. Loew received

Part Five: The Winters Years

his honor from the church, Holy Trinity added a new staff member. In 1977, James M. Bigham, Jr. became Director of Music. Thirty-six years later, Mr. Bigham continues to leave his mark on Holy Trinity's highly regarded music program. At the time Mr. Bigham joined Holy Trinity, discussions were underway concerning the future of the church's Möller pipe organ. The twenty-eight year old instrument was badly in need of repair. This would lead to yet another project within the sanctuary in the not-too-distant future.

A turnabout took place in 1977 as well. After the great blizzard, the church in Heilsburg, Germany, which Holy Trinity helped to build after World War II, sent a contribution to the Main Street church for victims of the snowstorm.

Discussions about the future of the Möller pipe organ also concluded in 1977. Experts who had been called to evaluate the instrument found that many of the organ's mechanical parts were badly deteriorated and would have to be replaced. The cost of this repair would be considerable. Enter Dr. Ralph Loew, who was the director of the Wendt Foundation. Through his efforts, a grant was obtained from that source for the repair, renovation, and additions to Holy Trinity's existing organ.

By January 1978, the chancel portion of the instrument had been installed. Following this step in the organ rebuilding, a series of recitals was held at Holy Trinity to dedicate this portion of the project. James Bigham, the church's own gifted organist, began the concert series. His performance was followed by recitals given by Frederick Swann of Manhattan's Riverside Church and Daniel Roth of Paris. Then a reunion concert took place with the return of Dr. Roberta Bitgood and John Becker, both former music directors at Holy Trinity. The 1979 history of the church terms this concert "a joyous homecoming" for both.

The English Evangelical Lutheran Church of the Holy Trinity reached a monumental milestone in 1979 celebrating its 100th anniversary in the city of Buffalo. The theme for this important occasion in the life of the Main Street church was a verse from a poem by Vachel Lindsay:

"This is our faith tremendous
Our wild hope, who shall scorn,
That in the name of Jesus
The world shall be reborn."

A centennial committee led by Dr. and Mrs. Kenneth H. Eckhert planned a busy calendar of events for 1979. The schedule included an Arts, Crafts, and Hobby Fair, an inaugural concert for the gallery organ, symposiums with Dr. Edgar Trexler and Dr. Martin Marty, a service celebrating the 25th anniversary of Pastor Matthew Winter's ordination, a Sunday School musical production, a 100th anniversary service, and a 100th anniversary banquet.

The Centennial Committee also oversaw the creation of a centennial gift. The goal: to raise at least $100,000 in order to create the "Loew Fund". Named to honor Dr. Ralph Loew, the fund would serve four purposes: Educational Outreach, Scholarly Outreach, Social Outreach, and Musical Outreach. The effort by co-Chairs, Stephen C. Ames and Thomas M. Barney, maintained Holy Trinity's tradition of reaching beyond its own walls to strengthen the church within.

Holy Trinity's 100th Anniversary celebration began with a festival service on May 6, 1979. This event was attended by clergy from across Western New York and New

Brass quintet playing at the 100th anniversary of Holy Trinity

York State – among them, Rabbi Martin L. Goldberg from Temple Beth Zion and The Rev. James M. Demske, S.J., president of Canisius College. Representatives from other churches and the community at large were in attendance as well – including individuals representing Buffalo Mayor James Griffin and Erie County Executive Edward Rutkowski. The master of ceremonies for the service was Ronald Leiser.

The music for the festival anniversary service was specially selected. On hand to further the tradition of excellent music at Holy Trinity was the church's Senior Choir, Youth Choir, and a brass choir of trumpets, French horns, trombones, tuba and percussion.

The festival procession entered the church to the hymn, "Ye Watchers and Ye Holy Ones" (LBW Hymn 175):

Pastor Matthew Winters during the 100th anniversary celebration.

> **"Ye watchers and ye holy ones**
> **Bright seraphs, cherubim, and thrones,**
> **Raise the glad strain:**
> **"Alleluia!"**

Following the singing of "A Mighty Fortress is our God," Dr. Ralph Loew gave the sermon. It was titled "*This Faith Tremendous: Overture To The Future.*" In his address, Dr. Loew likened the first 100 years of Holy Trinity to the overture of an opera . . . the beginning of the story.

The centennial celebration of Holy Trinity continued with an anniversary party on May 20, 1979 at the Statler Hilton Hotel in Buffalo. This joyous event involved a social hour, dinner, a skit titled "It Was Ever Thus" and dancing. Mr. Arthur Pellnat was the toastmaster for the evening. George Kline, president of the Church Council, and Dr. Kenneth

Part Five: The Winters Years

Eckhert, chairman of the 100th Anniversary Committee, each offered greetings at the event.

To cap the anniversary celebration, *This Faith Tremendous*, a book chronicling the 100 year history of Holy Trinity, was published. Written by Dr. Ralph Loew, Mrs. Kenneth Eckhert, Sr., and David M. Hehr, *This Faith Tremendous* was the second history of the Main Street church now in print. In the foreword of the book, Dr. Loew wrote:

> *"This is the story of a congregation, a community of believers whose persistent imaginative faith has witnessed in Buffalo and then shared in creative ministries throughout the world...."*

Pastor Matthew Winters wrote the epilogue for the book. In his essay, Pastor Winters commented:

> *"To march by a century mark, as we are doing in these days of 1979, is an exhilarating thing. We know that we cannot offer sufficient thanks for the guidance and power which the Holy Spirit has given to our predecessors. Praise be to God, ours is a rich heritage of vision, faith, and living service.*
>
> *But after 100 years, we do not simply thank God for how good He used to be. We are mindful of His continuing, abiding presence. And we must promise Him our loyalty and dedication afresh."*

Pastor Winters concludes his remarks with these sentiments:

> *"My hope and prayer is that we may bring to the future of Holy Trinity those qualities which have lent greatness*

to the past – deep faith in Christ; the conviction that His way is ours; a caring, generous feeling for our fellow human beings in our city, our nation, our world; and the willingness, yes, the desire to let God guide us at all times. If we do this, He will do the rest."

Holy Trinity's centennial celebration proved to be a joyous, inspiring time in the life of the church. Seven months after this milestone was observed a new decade began. In 1980, Ronald Reagan was elected the 40th President of the United States and ushered in a new era of conservatism. In that same year, Holy Trinity began its second century on Main Street in the city of Buffalo.

In April of 1980, *This Faith Tremendous*, the book about Holy Trinity's 100-year history, was published. In June of that year, as part of an international observance, Holy Trinity celebrated the 450th anniversary of the Augsburg Confession — the basis of what it means to be a Lutheran. Copies of the Augsburg Confession were made available to the congregation, study groups were organized, and a special service was held on October 5 to celebrate the anniversary. The service was sponsored by the Lutheran churches of the Niagara Frontier and the local Roman Catholic Diocese. Dr. Martin Marty preached at the event and Bishop Edward Head was a participant.

In the fall of 1980, Holy Trinity, in the tradition of a project undertaken in 1976, sponsored a second Laotian family. At this same time, a change in the church's Holy Communion schedule was under consideration. During this period in Holy Trinity's history, Holy Communion was offered at both the 8:30 and 10:30 services on the first Sunday of every month. In May of 1981, a "slight" change was made to Holy Trinity's communion schedule. Now, Holy Communion would be distributed on the first Sunday of every month at the 10:30 service and on the third Sunday of each month at the 8:30 service.

May of 1981 also saw the observance of a joyous occasion as the 50th anniversary of Dr. Ralph Loew's ordination as a Lutheran pastor was celebrated. Other noteworthy happenings from 1981 include the formation of handbell choirs and the first tour of the Margaret L. Wendt Memorial Organ.

In the fall of 1981, Holy Trinity's pattern of opening its arms to those in need emerged once more as the Sunday School children of Redeemer Lutheran Church were transported to Holy Trinity so they could be a part of the Main Street church's more active Sunday School program. To keep this relationship strong, a representative from Redeemer Church was added to the Christian Education Committee.

Early in 1982, a milestone was observed and a project was proposed at Holy Trinity. On February 7, recognition of the 10th anniversary of Trinity Tower was observed at the 10:30 service, followed by an open house and coffee hour in the Tower itself. During the same month, it was announced that the present organ console in the church needed to be replaced. The Church Council of Holy Trinity accepted an offer from the Margaret L. Wendt Foundation for the installation, at no cost, of two brand new solid state organ consoles, and layout plans were begun for the project.

A significant moment took place at Holy Trinity in the fall of 1982 when Pastor Joachim Wilck left the Main Street church. The Church Council named a committee to find Pastor Wilck's replacement. In time, the results of this search would have a powerful impact on the future of Holy Trinity.

In March of 1983, work began on the installation of two new organ consoles to the Margaret L. Wendt Memorial Organ. In time, these additions to the instrument would make it the largest and most comprehensive in the area.

Three other significant events took place at Holy Trinity in 1983. The first event occurred on September 24 of that year when "Young" Matthew Winters married Victoria Heath. The second event happened in October when Holy Trinity celebrated the Martin Luther Jubilee: the 500th anniversary of the great reformer's birth. To commemorate this milestone, Holy Trinity held special jubilee services on Reformation Sunday, offered a Monday morning Bible study series devoted to the life of Martin Luther and the Book of Romans, and showed the film, "Where Luther Walked." Also, Pastor Matthew Winters and Dr. Ralph Loew attended "Martin Luther Jubilee Week" in Washington, D.C. While in the nation's capital, Dr. Loew offered the opening prayer at a session of the U.S. Congress.

The third event, which also occurred in October of 1983, was important in the life of Holy Trinity and would take on an even greater significance nine years later. During the same month as the Luther jubilee, the Rev. Charles D. Bang accepted a call to become the associate pastor of Holy Trinity Lutheran Church. Pastor Bang came to the Main Street church after serving three years as pastor of King of Kings Lutheran Church in Liverpool, New York. A graduate of Hartwick College and Pacific Lutheran Seminary in Berkeley, California, 29-year-old Charles Bang and his wife, Deborah, arrived in Western New York with a plan, according to *Our Church Paper*, to "be living in the city of Buffalo, as close to the church as possible." In his first letter to the congregation of Holy Trinity, the new associate pastor wrote:

Part Five: The Winters Years

". . . . We come to Holy Trinity in the fall, and appropriately so, for in many ways, the leaves of our lives are also changing. We leave a community of loving, caring, sincere people of God, people with whom we have laughed and cried, played and prayed. It was a season in our lives, in many ways a spring and summer. But autumn does and must come and in many ways, there is winter, also. But spring looms in the future for us. We anticipate the budding, the new life, the promise of growth, a new summer. We leave one loving community and come to another, to that part of the Church of Jesus Christ that calls itself the First English Evangelical Lutheran Church of the Holy Trinity."

On January 8, 1984, Pastor Charles D. Bang was installed as associate pastor of Holy Trinity at a special service held on the first Sunday after the Epiphany – a day commemorating The Baptism of Our Lord. Nine days after Pastor Bang's installation, the inaugural recital of the newly enlarged Margaret L. Wendt Memorial Organ was held at Holy Trinity featuring James Bigham, organist and choir director of the church.

In the spring of 1984, the Lutheran Church Women of the Main Street church reorganized their association. During this time, the "LCW," on a national level, revised its constitution. On a local level, the LCW of Holy Trinity adopted the new constitution and reorganized into two circles as required by the new directive. They were known as the Daytime Circle and the Evening Circle. In this new form, women's programs at Holy Trinity would continue to be strong and active within the church.

In the fall of 1984, an important visitor came to Holy Trinity to present the congregation a proposal that would, in time, change Lutheranism in America. Dr. Edward K. Perry, Bishop of the Upper New York Synod of the Lutheran Church in America, visited Holy Trinity on November 11 to discuss the proposed merger of three major Lutheran Church bodies in the U.S.: The Association of Evangelical Lutheran Churches, the American Lutheran Church, and the Lutheran Church in America. Dr. Perry introduced the congregation to the task force that was formed to explore the possibility of uniting the three church bodies, the "Commission for a New Lutheran Church," and discussed that group's current activities.

A new year arrived at Holy Trinity, and with it a new program. Initiated by the church's Evangelism Committee, 1985 was proclaimed "The Year of the Visitor" at the Main Street church. Announcements in "Our Church Paper" encouraged members to bring a friend to church and to ". . . . Remember to honor all guests with a special bookmarker available at each guest register . . . ."

In March of 1985, Elizabeth Winters, the wife of Pastor Winters, was a recipient of the Council of Churches Appreciation Award for her dedicated work at Holy Trinity and in the Western New York community. During that same spring, Holy Trinity's Lutheran Church Women joined in an effort being led by the members of the Upper New York Synod LCW. The Lutheran Church Women of Upstate New York initiated the "Phebe Hospital Project" sending much needed supplies to the Phebe Hospital in Monrovia, Liberia. The women of Holy Trinity did their part as they collected and forwarded items to fulfill an important need at this African medical facility.

Part Five: The Winters Years

Nineteen eighty-five continued to be a time of pursuing projects at Holy Trinity. In the fall of the year, the Buffalo Chapter of Habitat for Humanity was formed. Dr. Ralph Loew was instrumental in bringing this organization to Buffalo. The Buffalo Chapter of Habitat held its initial meetings at Holy Trinity.

A sad moment took place in 1985 when one of Holy Trinity's "daughters," The Lutheran Church of the Redeemer, was closed. Some members of Redeemer Church joined the mother church, prompting Pastor Charles Bang to write,

". . . . Where God closes a door, He opens a window. We, among many others, have been blessed by the "dispersion" of Redeemer members into our midst. In dying, there is rising . . . ."

It is interesting to recall that Holy Trinity's parish hall was given a new name at this time. It was renamed "Redeemer Hall" in honor of the daughter church that unfortunately had to close its doors.

Early in 1986, a festival of three concerts was held to celebrate the completion of work done to enhance the Margaret L. Wendt Memorial Organ. The series began with a solo performance by Holy Trinity organist James Bigham. The subsequent concerts featured organist John Walker and Frederick Swann, organist of the Crystal Cathedral in California.

In February 1986, the Pastoral Relations Committee, which was organized to work with then Associate Pastor Charles Bang, published an interesting commentary in Holy Trinity's church paper. The committee had asked members of the congregation for feedback about Pastor Bang and his ministry at the Main Street church. The response the committee received was both very positive and very foretelling . . . .

> "*. . . . By far the majority of those responding find Pastor Bang warm, loving, outgoing, concerned, sensitive to people's needs, and blessed with a good sense of humor. They like his sermons, his reaching out to people, and his committee interest and involvement. They feel he relates well to all ages and is an asset to Holy Trinity, and they hope he'll be with us for a long time . . . .*"

Some routine maintenance was done to a portion of Holy Trinity's property in 1986 when the church's north parking lot was repaved. This particular moment in the life of the Main Street church may not seem to have much historical significance, but it does provide an interesting footnote.

The north parking lot of Holy Trinity is repaved every three years for very good reason. Back in time, the Haller house, the home of prominent Holy Trinity member Frederick Haller, stood on what is now the location of the church's north parking area. At some point, the Haller house burned and the debris from it was bulldozed into the ground. Over time, the debris began to decompose. This caused the ground, where the north parking lot was constructed, to sink. In order to keep the pavement in good condition, the north parking area has to be repaved every three years.

The first word of a possible merger of three American Lutheran Church bodies came to Holy Trinity in 1984. In February 1987, a fact sheet about the forthcoming new

Part Five: The Winters Years

church body, the Evangelical Lutheran Church in America, was published in *Our Church Paper*. The merger, now a reality, was slated to take effect on January 1, 1988.

In 1987, as the beginning of a new era in American Lutheranism was approaching, projects were going on at Holy Trinity. The refurbishing of the Fireside Room began, the Lutheran Church Women organized a prayer chain, and the congregation purchased a hearing aid system.

The hearing aid system, which is still in use at Holy Trinity today, works on the principle of radio broadcasting. A transmitter transmits the service which is picked up by a receiving device. The receiving device is equipped with an earphone and volume control. Since its introduction at Holy Trinity in 1987, this audio system has been highly successful and beneficial for those in the congregation who use it.

On January 1, 1988, the new Evangelical Lutheran Church in America (ELCA) began, and with it came some changes. The youth organization at Holy Trinity had been known as the Fellowship of Lutheran Youth (FLY). Now, all youth in ELCA churches would be united by a common identity: they would be members of the Lutheran Youth Organization (LYO). The Lutheran Church Women (LCW) took on a new identity as well. With the merger they became WELCA: Women of the Evangelical Lutheran Church in America.

A new processional cross was used at Holy Trinity for the first time on Easter Sunday 1988. It replaced a processional cross that had been given to church in 1952 by Carol Feltes in memory of her fiancé who died in World War II. The 1988 cross, designed by artist Chris Den Blaker, was also given to Holy Trinity by Carol Feltes. A pair of torches which accompany the cross were given to the church by Dr. and Mrs. Kenneth Eckhert, Jr. The new cross was commemorated on Holy Cross Day, September 14, 1988.

Transitions and milestones took place during 1988 in the life of the Main Street church. In May of the year, long-time caretaker of Holy Trinity, Otto Rosin, husband of Lilli, passed away. Otto had been associated with the parish for 34 years at the time of his death. A look at the July/August 1988 *Our Church Paper* reveals some exciting news. In that issue, Holy Trinity's choir announced plans for a European tour in 1989. In October 1988, Associate Pastor Charles Bang celebrated the fifth anniversary of his ministry at Holy Trinity.

In recognition of Charles Bang's work, dedication, and contributions to the life of the English Evangelical Lutheran Church of the Holy Trinity, the Church Council, at its September 1988 meeting, passed a resolution. Upon a motion by Pastor Matthew Winters, the word "Associate" was dropped from Pastor Bang's title. From that moment on, Charles D. Bang would have the title of "Pastor" at Holy Trinity Lutheran Church.

The year 1989 arrived and with it another milestone in the life of the Main Street church: Holy Trinity, the cathedral church of English Lutheranism in Western New York, celebrated its 110th anniversary. To commemorate this important occasion, the Social Ministries Committee recommended to the Church Council that Holy Trinity's congregation celebrate this anniversary by providing funds and manpower to renovate a house for Habitat For Humanity. The Church Council enthusiastically gave its approval.

The kickoff of this project took place at the coffee hour on the First Sunday After the Epiphany, January 8,

Part Five: The Winters Years

1989. Construction of a model house made out of popsicle sticks was begun at this event. Money donated to the Habitat House Project provided windows, doors, a roof, a chimney, plumbing and an interior – not to mention more popsicle stick siding – for the model house.

By April of 1989, lawyers were finalizing the closing for the Habitat house that members of Holy Trinity Church would be renovating. The house was located on Northampton Street in Buffalo. The 3rd and 4th grade Sunday School classes joined the effort at this time, raising funds for the rehabilitation of the walls of the building.

At the time of the closing on the Habitat house, an announcement was made at Holy Trinity: the church was going to have a new rear entrance with handicap access. The redecorating of the Fireside Room was also completed at this time.

On June 4, 1989, a blessed and joyous event happened at Holy Trinity: Dr. Ralph Loew, pastor emeritus, and his wife, Maxine Loew, celebrated their 50th wedding anniversary. Their daughters, Carolyn and Janet, and their families invited members and friends of Holy Trinity to join in the celebration by attending a festival service and reception at the Main Street church. The Rev. Dr. John W. Vannorsdall, president of the Lutheran Theological Seminary at Philadelphia preached at the event.

Shortly after the Loew's anniversary celebration, the choir of Holy Trinity Lutheran Church embarked on a 15-day concert tour of Europe. Leaving on June 24, the choir traveled through Poland, East Germany, and West Germany. They returned to Buffalo on July 7, 1989. Organist James Bigham recalls that "things were in a fever pitch in that part of the world — we didn't know it."

The concert tour began in Poland. While in Warsaw, the Holy Trinity Choir performed with the Warsaw Philharmonic Orchestra. This was an impressive event as the choir of the Main Street Lutheran church in Buffalo was the first of its kind to perform with one of the Polish State orchestras before an era of change swept Europe after the fall of the Berlin Wall (an event that happened only a few months later).

The choir traveled from Warsaw, Poland to Leipzig, East Germany during the first week of their tour. This part of the journey included an emphasis on the "Luther Lands." The choir visited Eisleben, Martin Luther's birthplace, the castle church in Wittenberg where Martin Luther is buried (it is also the site where the great reformer posted his 95 theses), and other places.

On Sunday, July 2, 1989, the choir participated in Sunday worship at the famous St. Thomas Church. This is the parish where Johann Sebastian Bach spent much of his career and the site where he is buried.

Back in 1947, the congregation of Holy Trinity helped to build a church in Heilsburg, West Germany with a gift of $10,000. Forty-two years later, while on the 1989 tour, the choir of Holy Trinity sang in the same Heilsburg church the congregation helped to build. "It was quite an emotional thing," said organist James Bigham. In commemoration of the aforementioned 1947 gift, Holy Trinity Church is depicted in one of the stained glass windows of the Heilsburg church.

On July 7, 1989, the choir of Holy Trinity boarded a plane in Frankfurt, West Germany and made the journey back to Buffalo, ending an exciting, emotional, and successful tour. In the June 1989 issue of *Our Church Paper* the following mission statement was made prior to this trip to Europe:

"As representatives of Holy Trinity Church, the choir hopes to serve as ambassadors for Christ through a ministry of music which crosses all barriers . . . ."

From all accounts, this is exactly what the musicians from Holy Trinity accomplished on their tour.

The second half of 1989 was a time of projects devoted to maintenance of the interior and exterior of the church. By September of the year, all twenty stained glass ventilators in the sanctuary had been replaced. The original iron-framed vents had become difficult, and, in some cases, impossible, to close completely. This caused a loss of heat from the main sanctuary which led to discomfort for congregants. While the ventilators were being replaced, all 20 clerestory windows in the sanctuary were cleaned and repaired. Both of these tasks were undertaken and completed by the McHugh Art Studio.

The September 1989 *Our Church Paper* announced two other projects for the fall of 1989: a new roof would be put on the Sunday School portion of the building and approval was given for the construction of a new side door near the front of the church.

In November 1989, another change to Holy Trinity's Holy Communion schedule was announced by the Worship Committee. Beginning on January 1, 1990, Holy Communion would take place on the first and third Sundays of each month at the 10:30 service in the main sanctuary. In the Mansperger Chapel, Holy Communion would take place on the second and fourth Sundays of each month. The Worship Committee followed their announcement of the new schedule with these words:

"We hope the initial confusion over this new schedule will quickly ease and everyone will come to share the Lord's table on more frequent occasions."

The English Evangelical Lutheran Church of the Holy Trinity entered the 1990s keeping with its tradition of engaging in projects beyond its own walls. The year 1990 began with a project mounted by the Holy Trinity Sunday School. In January, the Sunday School began collecting pennies to raise funds for the church's Habitat For Humanity project. In all, the Sunday School children raised $500 which paid for wiring in the Habitat house.

Early in 1990, events were planned to heighten awareness of and knowledge about issues of national and worldwide importance. In February, Holy Trinity hosted a seminar about AIDS. On March 31, 1990, the "Lutherans Love The Earth" Educational Conference About the Environment was held at Holy Trinity. Eight Lutheran congregations from the Western New York area were represented at this event.

In June of 1990, Church Council President David Ulrich announced a change in Holy Trinity's church year from a fiscal (July to June) to a calendar year (January to December) basis. The effect of this change would mainly be on the Church Council's budgetary process.

The autumn of 1990 was a busy time at Holy Trinity. On September 23, the Main Street church hosted the 5th anniversary celebration of Habitat For Humanity/Buffalo. Included in this event was an organ prelude by organist James Bigham, a festival service, and a festive reception.

On October 13, 1990, the Christian Education Committee sponsored a "Career Day" for Lutheran high school students. It should be noted that all ELCA congregations within the Niagara Frontier were invited to participate in this day of education and awareness. In *Our Church Paper*, the Christian Education Committee said,

> *"The purpose of this event will be to inform our youth and their parents of the educational opportunities available at Lutheran colleges and universities in this country as well as the employment opportunities available in the church."*

Workshops on resume writing, interviewing skills, college application writing, and scholarships were held as part of this community-oriented event.

In the wake of the change in Holy Trinity's Holy Communion schedule came another change in the worship "schedule" at the church. In the fall of 1990, the Worship Committee decided to use the second setting of the Service of Holy Communion. The committee felt it was important that the congregation become familiar with either Setting One or Setting Two. (The church had generally used Setting Three.) A strong influence on this change was that both Settings One and Two were being used by many other Lutheran churches. *Our Church Paper* reported that Setting Two of the Lutheran liturgy would be used at both Sunday services for a six month period from October 7, 1990 through March 31, 1991. Attached to this change was a long-range plan: that Holy Trinity would use Setting Two for half of the year and Setting Three for the other half. In time, this long-range plan would be carried out.

Finally, in the fall of 1990, in *Our Church Paper* an exciting announcement was made: that almost $10,000 had been raised over a 14-month period for Holy Trinity's Habitat house at 306 Northampton Street in Buffalo. In addition to this news, Holy Trinity's publication also reported that work on the Habitat house was under way and that a family had been chosen to live in the dwelling.

Nineteen ninety-one began at Holy Trinity with an announcement that foretold of changes soon to come in the pastorate of the Main Street church. Pastor Matthew Winters made it known in January that he would be retiring from the ministry sometime in 1992.

The women of Holy Trinity continued to be agents of change. When members of the congregation received their copy of the March 1991 *Our Church Paper*, they were greeted with a strikingly different publication. This issue was the first to be produced on a computer using word processing technology. Marge Barney volunteered to "computerize" the church paper and took the 100-year-old publication into a new era. During that same March, Susan Saur became the first woman to serve as an usher at Holy Trinity on a regularly scheduled basis.

In June 1991, a joyous celebration occurred when the Buffalo Chapter of Habitat For Humanity dedicated "The Holy Trinity House" at 306 Northampton Street in Buffalo. This event involved a dedication ceremony, tours of the house, and a reception. Members of the congregation, children of the Sunday School, and friends of Holy Trinity contributed more than $10,000 to a very worthwhile and highly successful endeavor. Once again, the tradition of pursuing projects for "the care and redemption" of God's creation was maintained by the congregation of the Main Street church.

The autumn of 1991 was a time to look to the future

of Holy Trinity. On Sunday, November 17, a congregational meeting was held. At that gathering, the congregation overwhelmingly voted to empower the Church Council to issue a call to Charles D. Bang to become the sixth senior pastor of the English Evangelical Lutheran Church of the Holy Trinity. Pastor Bang's call would take effect on October 26, 1992. In this twenty-minute meeting, the congregation had begun to write the next chapter in its 112-year history.

On October 25, Reformation Sunday 1992, Pastor Matthew Littleton Winters delivered his final sermon and officially retired as senior pastor of Holy Trinity Lutheran Church. This event culminated nearly four decades of distinguished and faithful service by Pastor Winters to the Lutheran Church – six of those as associate pastor and 17 years as senior pastor at Holy Trinity.

Immediately after the 10:45 a.m. service, the congregation was invited to a reception for Matthew and Elizabeth Winters. During that event, the Winters were presented with a memory book that was made especially for them, and Pastor Winters offered words of thanks and appreciation to the congregation.

In the January 1993 issue of *Our Church Paper*, a message of gratefulness from Matthew and Elizabeth Winters was published. Among the sentiments in the message was the following:

". . . St. Paul said it frequently: "I thank God upon every remembrance of you." . . . Elizabeth and I join in saying about you, the members of Holy Trinity, "We thank God upon every remembrance of you." . . . The years have been filled with personal response but, especially during this past October, there was literally a deluge of

delight. The attendance on Reformation Sunday, the very generous gifts, the cards and personal words, the assurance of your prayers and concern for our future . . . for all these, we give thanks.

Now, we turn to a new chapter. It's a new beginning for you, the members of Holy Trinity, and for your Pastor, Charles Bang and his family, and certainly it is a new one for Elizabeth and me. Be assured we will never forget you in our heart and in our prayers. Hopefully, in the future, we will be able to serve in some way with you in the work of Christ's mission and ministry as He continues to use Holy Trinity here in the heart of Buffalo.

So . . . to each and everyone of you, and to our Lord Jesus Christ who through his love and overwhelming grace has made all these wonderful years possible, 'We thank God upon every remembrance.'"

The Rev. Dr. Matthew L. Winters left an enduring impression on Holy Trinity Lutheran Church. His "theology" is expressed in these words from his own message in *Our Church Paper* of February, 1992:

"It doesn't matter how many or how expensive, or whether you get any valentines at all. God loves you. God cares for you. You are important to Him . . . ."

The ministry of Matthew Winters was important to Holy Trinity.

Part Six: The Bang Years
1992 to the Present

"Beautiful Savior,
King of creation,
Son of God and Son of Man!
Truly I'd love thee,
Truly I'd serve thee,
Light of my soul, my joy, my crown."

LBW Hymn 518

Reverend Charles D. Bang the sixth pastor of Holy Trinity

On October 26, 1992, a new era dawned on the English Evangelical Lutheran Church of the Holy Trinity. On this day, Charles Douglas Bang became the sixth senior pastor in the 113-year history of the Main Street church. It should be noted that this was only the second time that an associate pastor was "promoted" to the rank of senior pastor at Holy Trinity. The first time happened 65 years earlier when Dr. Henry Pflum became senior pastor when Dr. Frederick Kahler retired in 1927. In the January 1992 issue of "Our Church Paper" Congregation President James Dunnigan wrote a letter to the congregation in which he anticipated the change that lay ahead in Holy Trinity's pastorate. Of the "new" senior pastor, Dunnigan wrote:

> "... *As we reflect, we also anticipate with celebration for the gift of ministry we are able to witness. Pastor Bang has demonstrated the truth of his call and his sincere desire to serve. The strength and power of his faith brought him to the position of Senior Pastor. Our support and participation will enable his growth to the rarified levels of his predecessors.*
>
> *Continue to celebrate and sing the carols and hymns of this wonderful Christmas season. Also plan to celebrate this year of transition; sing with your deepest commitment and anticipation the gifts of the ministry which are yet to be unwrapped ..."*

The installation of Pastor Bang took place on Christ the King Sunday, November 22, 1992. Only one service was held that day – Sunday School and Adult Education did not meet.

Preservice music began at 10:45 a.m., and the service at 11:00 a.m. The installing officer was the Rev. Paul R. Mertzlufft, dean of the Niagara Frontier Conference, the Upstate New York Synod of the Evangelical Lutheran Church in America. The sermon was given by Holy Trinity Pastor Emeritus Ralph W. Loew. Two other pastors and ten members of the congregation also participated in the service.

During the installation, Pastor Bang was led to the

baptismal font, the pulpit, and the altar of the church. At each location, he was "reminded" of his call to the ministry and the pastorate of Holy Trinity. After this solemn yet festive event, a reception and luncheon were held in Redeemer Hall in honor of Pastor and Mrs. Bang.

In the December 1992 issue of *Our Church Paper*, Charles Bang published his first column as Holy Trinity's senior pastor. In his remarks, Pastor Bang wrote:

> *"... For us then, let us be reminded of the Good News of Advent: That God sent to us a Son, born of woman, so that we would know that God knows what it is like to be human, to feel pain, to endure suffering, to say good-bye to friends. So that when this Son died, and when this Child was raised, it would be in the realm of our comprehension that the very same is promised and possible for us...."*

December 1992 was a busy music month at Holy Trinity. On December 4 through 6, a production of Giancarlo Menotti's Christmas classic, "Amahl and the Night Visitors," was staged by Holy Trinity and The Greater Buffalo Opera Company. This 50 minute opera was composed in 1951 for NBC Television. This joint production featured James Bigham at the organ, the Holy Trinity Choir, and the Holy Trinity Youth Choir. Members of the Holy Trinity Choir appeared in some of the principal roles.

Then, on December 18 and 19, 1992, the Holy Trinity Choir performed again – this time at Kleinhans Music Hall. The choir of the Main Street church collaborated with the Buffalo Philharmonic Orchestra on a presentation of G. F. Handel's oratorio, "The Messiah."

On Saturday, March 13, 1993, a major weather event affected much of the eastern United States, and Buffalo, New York would not escape its wrath. The Blizzard of 1993 or "The Storm of the Century," as the American news media called it, hit Buffalo on March 13 dumping nearly two feet of snow over the Western New York area. Holy Trinity held regular worship services on Sunday, March 14. Four staff members, including Pastor Bang, made it to the church. Three people — Dave, Pat and son, David Ulrich, attended the 8:30 a.m. service. Twelve people attended the 10:45 a.m. service. As always, the doors of the Main Street church were open to the faithful who braved the elements.

For many years, Holy Trinity had been a center of social activism in the city of Buffalo. In April 1993, that tradition would continue as the Niagara Frontier Conference of Women of the ELCA held their annual spring assembly at Holy Trinity. The theme of this event, which would be heard again at the Main Street church, was environmentalism. Called "The Green Spirit," this event reminded those in attendance that Christians must be stewards of the earth.

In spring 1993, another event was held at Holy Trinity that would begin yet another tradition that continues to this day: the first Chiavetta's chicken barbecue took place to benefit Habitat for Humanity. Currently, the Main Street church stages this event every September.

In the autumn of 1993, Holy Trinity celebrated the 15th anniversary of its concert series. The "kick-off" performance of this celebration was given by Frederick L. Swann, organist of the Crystal Cathedral of Garden Grove, California. Concerts continued later in 1993 and in the winter and spring of 1994 upholding yet another important tradition at Holy Trinity.

Also in October 1993, the Women of the ELCA at Holy Trinity sponsored "Blanket Sunday" to raise contributions that would buy blankets to be distributed by the Church World Service to people in need around the world. In all, the Women of the ELCA at Holy Trinity received enough donations to purchase over 150 blankets. Less than a week later, the Main Street church welcomed Dr. Martin Marty, Distinguished Service Professor of the History of Modern Christianity at the University of Chicago, and Senior Editor of *The Christian Century*. Dr. Marty presented a workshop at Holy Trinity and preached at both Sunday services on October 17. It should be noted that this program was presented by Joint Educational Ministry, a cooperative effort by Holy Trinity Lutheran, Westminster Presbyterian, and Trinity Episcopal Churches.

Nineteen ninety - four dawned, and with it came the end of an era. On January 9 of that year, Concordia Lutheran, a "daughter" church of Holy Trinity, held its last worship service. The following Saturday, January 15, the congregation of Holy Trinity hosted a luncheon where members of Holy Trinity's Church Council and staff met with members of the Concordia congregation who had been invited to join the Main Street church. About a month later, 26 new members did join Holy Trinity – many of whom were from Concordia Lutheran.

A significant event took place at Holy Trinity on May 8, 1994. "Ralph Loew Sunday" was held to celebrate Pastor Emeritus Loew's 50 years of ministry to Holy Trinity and the Western New York community. Dr. Loew preached, and a luncheon was hosted by Holy Trinity's Lutheran Youth Organization in honor of Dr. and Mrs. Loew.

The first major project undertaken by the Holy Trinity

congregation during Charles Bang's pastoral administration was unveiled in the June 1994 issue of *Our Church Paper*. At the time of this publication, the main sanctuary was approaching 90 years of age. The pews in the church were still the originals and many had deteriorated. The time had indeed come for the Main Street church to be renovated.

The "Vision Statement" published in the June 1994 church newsletter described the proposed renovation. The Church Council wanted the "valued appointments of the sanctuary" to be preserved. These facets of the main worship space included: the altar, pulpit, lectern, baptismal font, the windows in the balcony and the chancel, and the Tiffany window of the baptismal transept which was given to the church in 1905. As the vision statement expressed it:

"These traditional and worshipful appointments need to be enhanced by renovation of the sanctuary in keeping with their value and tradition."

The preliminary proposed renovation would involve the following: extending the chancel (altar and choir areas), installing a new floor for the chancel and nave of the church, refinishing the wainscot in a lighter color, installing new and more comfortable pews throughout the church, moving the pulpit and lectern to accommodate the extended chancel, updating and consolidating the lighting system, installing a new sound system, and, finally, installing an elevator in a place within the Holy Trinity complex so that all areas of the church would be accessible. This would be a major building renovation project dependent on the support demonstrated by the members of Holy Trinity Church.

By June 1994, a Renovation Committee had been

formed with David Schopp as its chair, and a study was launched by Cargill and Associates of Fort Worth, Texas, a consulting firm retained by the Holy Trinity Church Council to determine the feasibility of the renovation of the church. Two informational meetings were also held with the Holy Trinity congregation. The purpose of these gatherings was to inform the church membership about details of the project and to get feedback and suggestions from them about what ought to be included in the renovation. Questionnaires were made available to church members as well for written responses.

On June 29, 1994, a report was presented to the Holy Trinity Church Council about the results of the study. In the July/August 1994 issue of *Our Church Paper*, Pastor Bang reported that 75% of the project was deemed imperative, 20% of the renovation would be needed in 5 to 10 years, and 5% fell in the category of "it would be nice if we could....." Pastor Bang made this comment about the scope of the renovation.

"We ... realize that if our church is truly to be a center for our congregation's mission for the community, it needs to be a functional space for many other things...."

With all this groundwork completed, plans for the renovation of the Main Street church began to move forward.

In January 1995, the capital fund drive known as "A Firm Foundation" to finance the renovation of Holy Trinity was begun. In Phase I of this campaign, a goal was set to raise $260,000. By the spring of 1995, the congregation had exceeded that objective by nearly $30,000.

As the capital fund drive entered Phase II, plans

for the renovation continued. On Sunday May 7, 1995, the first of two coffee hours sponsored by the Renovation Committee took place. The reason for this gathering was to give members of the congregation the opportunity to ask questions about the status of the renovation and the various projects that were involved in it.

Three days after the first Renovation Committee coffee hour, an unexpected event occurred that would alter the entire renovation plan of Holy Trinity. On Wednesday, May 10, 1995, at about 6:35 p.m., the Main Street church was struck by lightning during a storm. Later inspection revealed that the location of the lightning strike was behind the Main Street façade of the church – almost directly behind the cross on the front of the building.

The outside of the church fortunately sustained minor damage. An area five feet by five feet was blown out of the back of the façade. The most serious consequence of the lightning strike was damage to electronic equipment inside the building. An intense magnetic field from the lightning was absorbed by wiring that connects the front and back organs in the main sanctuary of the church. The result was that major portions of the security and fire alarm system were destroyed. Two telephone lines and three video cameras were lost. The largest single item that sustained damage was Holy Trinity's organ itself. The intense magnetic field shorted out the solid state electronics of the instrument.

Before the organ was inspected, the fear was that a majority of the electronic components had been destroyed. In late May of 1995, Larry Hawkins, a representative of the Van Zoeran Organ Company, the firm that built Holy Trinity's instrument, came to Buffalo from Washington State to inspect the damage. The result was a "good news/bad news" report.

Part Six: The Bang Years — 1992 to the Present

The good news was that Mr. Hawkins was able to replace some of the damaged parts so that the organ could be played on a limited basis. The bad news was that the Margaret L. Wendt Memorial Organ had to be rebuilt. It was decided then that a major organ renovation would take place simultaneously with the scheduled renovation of the sanctuary.

The end of an article on the lightning strike in the June 1995 *Our Church Paper* showed that the result of this unfortunate event could have been worse.

> *"All things considered, we were very fortunate that the lightning struck where it did. Had it moved 8 inches lower, it would have hit the wood and shingle part of the church and in all likelihood would have caused a fire of major proportion. So, with gratitude, we say, "Thank God," and ask you for your continued prayers and patience until we get everything back in good order."*

On May 21, the second of two informational coffee hours sponsored by the Renovation Committee occurred after church services. Members of the congregation were given the status of the renovation, the ramifications of the lightning strike, and another opportunity to give feedback regarding the entire project.

In the spring of 1995, planning for the Holy Trinity renovation project took yet another turn when the Church Council decided to go ahead with the installation of the elevator — one of the most important additions to the parish campus. This action was taken even though the Firm Foundation campaign had not yet been completed. The first step toward construction of the elevator would involve the

Renovation Committee taking bids on this project in the summer of 1995.

While all the preliminary renovation planning was going on, the congregation of Holy Trinity, as it always had done, engaged in social outreach. By the spring of 1995, the Holy Trinity Christian Action Committee had made 4 quilts, knitted over 40 lap robes, and constructed 58 health kits. The health kits filled over 123 cartons! Most of the aforementioned items were sent to Lutheran World Relief. Twelve health kits were distributed locally. Once again, the congregation of the Main Street church continued its long tradition of extending its Christian commitment across the globe.

Autumn of 1995 came and with it news that pledges to the Firm Foundation campaign for the renovation project had exceeded $300,000. During this same season, the Women of the ELCA at Holy Trinity presented an Oktoberfest in Redeemer Hall with all the appropriate German trimmings: sausage, beer, and a German band named The Frankfurters.

The November 1995 *Our Church Paper*, along with staff contact information, announced that Holy Trinity, for the first time ever, had its own "e-mail" address. With this advancement, the Main Street church, in its 116th year, took another step into cyberspace.

By December of 1995, the elevator portion of the renovation project was well under way. Dover Elevator Company and Grandview Construction Company had been enlisted to build the elevator and its shaft. This new mode of "transportation" within the Holy Trinity campus would provide access to the three levels of the building (the basement, the main church, and the Sunday School).

Construction of the elevator continued during the winter months of the new year.

On Saturday evening, December 9 and Sunday, December 10, 1995, the city of Buffalo and part of its metropolitan area were hit by a lake effect winter storm. The result was a 38.7 inch snowfall in one 24-hour period. On December 10, 1995, Mayor Anthony Masiello declared a state of emergency in the Buffalo city limits and issued a driving ban. True and faithful to its mission, Holy Trinity had Advent worship services at 8:30 a.m. and 10:30 a.m. that morning in spite of the snowy weather. In his January 1996 message to the congregation, Pastor Bang paid tribute to the 13 parishioners who made it to the 8:30 service and the 35 who came to the 10:30 worship. Pastor Bang referred to the faithful who braved the elements and came to church on December 10 as faithful "LEL's": 48 charter members of "The Holy Royal Order of Lake Effect Lutherans." Holy Trinity's sixth senior pastor summed up that snowy Sunday morning with these words:

"Veni, Vedi, Vesang — ve came, ve saw, ve had church."

Though a storm went on outside, thanks and praise to God continued inside the walls of the Main Street church.

The year 1996 dawned and with it, a presidential election cycle in the United States. At this time, the Women of the Evangelical Lutheran Church at Holy Trinity embarked on another in-gathering project which involved assembling school kits. School items such as writing pads, crayons, and rulers were put into the kits which were then sent overseas through Lutheran World Relief.

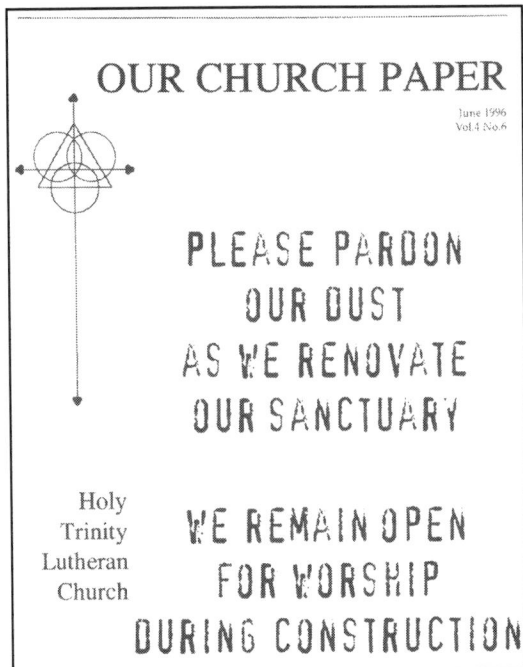

OUR CHURCH PAPER

June 1996
Vol.4 No.6

PLEASE PARDON
OUR DUST
AS WE RENOVATE
OUR SANCTUARY

Holy
Trinity
Lutheran
Church

WE REMAIN OPEN
FOR WORSHIP
DURING CONSTRUCTION

The cover of "Our Church Paper" of June 1996. This issue was published during the renovation of the sanctuary of Holy Trinity.

Early in 1996, work on the elevator continued and plans for the renovation gained momentum. By this time, the decision had been made to move worship services to Redeemer Hall after May 12 so that the renovation process could begin. The hope was that the main sanctuary would be ready for Christmas Eve 1996. At that time Congregation President, Ronald Leiser, a longtime member of Holy Trinity, put the renovation project and the mission of the church in perspective. In an article, published in the January 1996 issue of *Our Church Paper*, he wrote,

> *".....To complete this future vision, it is essential that we take care of the present. Yearly stewardship becomes increasingly important. Our treasure keeps this church, its ministry, and all its fine programs viable.*
>
> *The standards this church has set in preaching, teaching and music should never be lowered. As a downtown church, it is our duty to expand our social outreach deeper into the community."*

These comments by President Leiser illustrate the congregational mindset of the Main Street church – a spirit of service that has been alive within the leaders and stewards of Holy Trinity since its founding.

As winds of change to the Holy Trinity building were swirling throughout the church, other changes took place. On February 1, 1996, Lilli Rosin, the long-time helper and housekeeper for Holy Trinity, retired after 42 years of service to the church. On Sunday, February 18, she officially became a member of the congregation.

Sad news came to Holy Trinity on March 5, 1996, that its pastor from 1944 to 1975, Ralph W. Loew, had died while vacationing in Florida. He was 88 years old. Though Holy Trinity's pastor emeritus had been known and respected nationally and internationally, Dr. Loew had first and foremost been a parish pastor, and the events of his funeral, planned by him, were to take place within the Main Street parish he served for more than 31 years.

On March 16, 1996, a memorial service for Ralph Loew was held at Holy Trinity. The sanctuary was filled, and a large group of Western New York Lutheran clergy – many of whom claimed Ralph Loew as a mentor – attended and participated in the event. One local clergyman, Rabbi Emeritus Martin Goldberg of Temple Beth Zion in Buffalo, called Pastor Bang and asked to participate in the service. Rabbi Goldberg would deliver remarks of fond remembrance of his friend and colleague during Dr. Loew's memorial.

The front of the bulletin for Dr. Loew's tribute bore his favorite quotation from former Secretary General of the United Nations, Dag Hammerskjold:

"For all that has been – Thanks!
For all that will be – Yes!"

The sermon hymn for the day was "Abide With Me."
It concluded with the words:

"Hold thou thy cross before my closing eyes,
Shine through the gloom and point me to the skies,
Heav'n's morning breaks and earth's vain shadows flee,
In life, in death, O Lord, abide with me."
LBW Hymn 272

In his sermon, Pastor Charles Bang remembered
Holy Trinity's pastor emeritus in the following way:

"....If I could say something about Ralph Loew, I would
say that God was his closest friend; and he never missed
the opportunity to introduce him to anyone who came
under his roof or into his circle.
For the power of this great love he had for God and
for him introducing us to the great love God has for us,
for all these things, for all that has been – thanks!"

Also, in his eulogy, Pastor Bang told the congregation
what Dr. Loew wanted to happen on this day:

".....He wanted today to be a day of celebration and
sharing and storytelling.....More important than what
was to be said, was who was to be here, and that was
the essence of Ralph Loew. While he was quite specific
about what he wanted said at this service and who
would say it, while he told us which hymns he liked and

what choir music he liked, he was most explicit about the fact that people should be given the opportunity to visit with one another, and eat and talk and remember.

So, while your hearts may be heavy, if you want to do what Ralph wanted done most, don't let the heaviness of your hearts weigh down your vocal chords. The best tribute to this great man, at least on this day, will be to have a room full of people gathered together, telling stories, sharing life, celebrating each other…..”

At the reception in Redeemer Hall following Dr. Loew's memorial service that was exactly what took place: people visited with each other and ate and talked and remembered Holy Trinity's fourth senior pastor with great fondness.

In the spring of 1996, Holy Trinity's renovation plans continued to move forward. On May 12, Mother's Day, the last service in the main sanctuary was held. The church calendar was "advanced" to Pentecost on this day in order to have confirmation in the sanctuary. Otherwise, this important moment in the life of the church would have taken place down in Redeemer Hall on the true day of Pentecost. On May 19, the 10:30 service was, in fact, held in Redeemer Hall – the temporary sanctuary until the reopening of the main church on Christmas Eve of 1996. Pastor Bang at this time affectionately renamed Redeemer Hall "The Garden Level" of Holy Trinity. For church service on May 19, Pastor Bang selected "In the Garden" as the processional hymn – a fitting opening to the temporary setting for worship at the Main Street church.

After the May 12 worship service, work commenced on the removal, packing and storing of organ pipes in the main sanctuary of Holy Trinity. In this two week period leading up to the beginning of the renovation, the Margaret Wendt Memorial Organ was also removed for its rebuilding, and scaffolding was erected to enable the testing of paint colors on the upper reaches of the ceiling vaults.

Also in this two week period, members of Holy Trinity were offered the chance to acquire old pews from the main sanctuary. In the May 1996 *Our Church Paper*, the following comment about the "pew sale" appeared:

". . . The Memorial Day weekend was an end and a beginning . . . More than thirty pews were bought and many were the comments about how much bigger the pews became as we struggled to get them into a van or a truck and then wiggle them through doors and around corners at home . . ."

A $100 contribution to the Firm Foundation fund was suggested in exchange for one of the historic pews.

By May 28, 1996, all of the old pews were out of the sanctuary and the renovations of Holy Trinity's main church worship space had begun. Workers of the McHugh Painting contractors moved in and began removing carpeting.

The summer of 1996 came, and with it, the completion of the elevator project. It should be noted that when the elevator was installed, one restroom on the second floor of the church and two restrooms on the lowest level of the building were made handicap accessible. Two interesting discoveries were made during the elevator work as well. While the elevator was being installed a marble mosaic was uncovered in a section of the floor near the entrances to the church that lead to the front and rear parking lots and the

Part Six: The Bang Years — 1992 to the Present

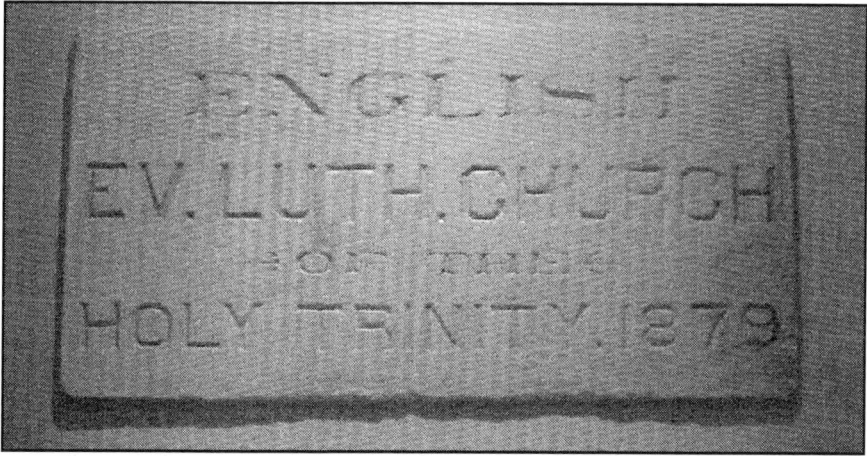

The cornerstone of the original Holy Trinity Church at Ellicott and Tupper streets. It was found by Pastor Bang during the 1996 renovation of the church.

chapel. The mosaic bears the intertwined initials "H.T." It is estimated that the mosaic had been covered for 60 years. No long-time living member remembered seeing it.

The second interesting find was discovered by Pastor Charles Bang himself. During the renovation, for insurance purposes, glass doors had to be installed in the entrance to the pastor's study. When he went to look for a glass door down in the church's furnace room, Pastor Bang found the cornerstone from the original Holy Trinity Lutheran Church that was located at the intersection of Ellicott and Tupper streets (Holy Trinity's sanctuary prior to 1905). The cornerstone was behind the church's furnaces and covered in coal dust. Naturally, the over 100-year-old cornerstone was taken out of its hiding place and installed as a monument to Holy Trinity's "founding era" where it could (and still can) be easily viewed. The cornerstone was installed in a wall right above the marble mosaic. It reads:

English
Ev. Luth. Church

of the
Holy Trinity, 1879

Throughout the summer of 1996, renovation work in the sanctuary went on swiftly and as scheduled. As changes began to take place in the building, changes also occurred in the congregation. On June 12, a long-time presence at Holy Trinity, Lilli Rosin, passed away. Along with her husband, Otto, she had been a caretaker of the church since the administration of Dr. Ralph Loew. During her long tenure at Holy Trinity, Lilli could often be seen working in the church kitchen. After her passing, Lilli was deeply missed by all who knew and cherished her.

About the changes going on at Holy Trinity, Congregation President Emerson Horner wrote:

" . . . Yes, the times are a-changin'. But in the midst of these changes, we can continue to rely on the unchanging grace of our Heavenly Father. As Pastor Bang often observes, change is the only sign of life. Indeed, life abounds at Holy Trinity. . . ."

By September the renovation project was right on schedule. By then, the ceiling in the nave – the main church – had been completed, plaster repairs and painting had been done, and new ceiling fans had been installed. In addition, the woodwork in the main sanctuary had been stripped and was in the process of being stained and refinished, and more elaborate painting on the ceiling of the chancel was underway.

Renovation Committee Chair David Schopp also reported that on September 15, 1996, Pastor Bang led a tour of the renovation project. Congregation members were taken into areas of the church that had been off-limits since the end of May. Virtually everyone on the tour was impressed by the way the painting in the sanctuary highlighted previously overlooked or obscured architectural details.

By October 1996, the renovation continued swiftly. The marble contractor, Giancarlo Giovannetti, had begun the work to reinstall the altar and lay the marble floor to the chancel. In addition, the painting of the nave was almost complete, and supplemental lighting in the church had been installed.

While the renovation moved ahead, other events took place in the life of the Main Street church. On November 3, 1996, Holy Trinity Lutheran Church and Trinity Episcopal Church held an ecumenical worship service in the sanctuary of Trinity Episcopal. Both church choirs participated and both congregations shared in a luncheon after the service. On November 15 through 17, the Joint Educational Ministry (known as JEM), a collaboration of Holy Trinity, Westminster Presbyterian and Trinity Episcopal, presented a program featuring the Reverend James R. Adams. While work went on in its own sanctuary, Holy Trinity continued to make an impact on religious life in the city of Buffalo.

With Christmas Eve 1996 drawing near, the renovation kept moving forward. By November of the year, the altar in the main sanctuary had been cleaned and reinstalled. It was now free-standing. This would allow clergy to stand behind the altar. Renovation Chair David Schopp wrote,

"... we believe the congregation will be pleased to see that adaptations have had little impact on the overall appearance of the altar...."

In time, this statement would prove to be true. During November 1996, work continued on the nave (congregation area) and chancel (altar and choir area) of Holy Trinity's main sanctuary. By this time, portions of the chancel floor, which had deteriorated over time, had been rebuilt and given stronger support. The marble around the altar had been cleaned and the marble floor and steps in the chancel had been installed.

After completion of the marble work, the entire floor of the nave was sanded, stained, and refinished, and carpeting was installed in the aisles. Other November projects included the refurbishing of the narthex (the vestibule between entrances to the building and the main sanctuary), the coatroom, and the hallway near the church office. In time, a memorial gallery was created for displaying paintings, other items of historical significance to Holy Trinity, and memorial plaques. Accent lighting was also installed in the gallery.

One other project was done in the area adjacent to the church office: the former LYO Room was turned into a sacristy for the church. All communion ware, altar linens, candles, worship assistant robes and other items needed for worship would now be stored in this room.

By Christmas Eve of 1996, most of the renovation project was done, and both services on December 24 were held in the main sanctuary. Pastor Bang, in the December issue of *Our Church Paper*, looked forward to the moment to come:

". . . . It's probably, most likely, hopefully, certainly the most expensive Christmas present we'll ever receive. On Christmas Eve, our sanctuary and nave will reopen after four years of planning, two years of

designing, and seven months (twelve if you add the elevator) of renovation work. . . . The congregation and community are to be commended; first, for their faithfulness in all things. Not the least of which include faithful stewardship, faithful attendance in Redeemer Hall (perhaps forever known as "The Garden Level"), and their faithful trust in those who orchestrated the renovation and the workers who accomplished it. Second, you are to be commended on your patience. With the last details being added to the room, we have not been allowed to let you inside the church. This has been a disappointment to some, but I believe we will be all the more surprised and pleased and excited come Christmas Eve. . . ."

Things got stressful at Holy Trinity before Christmas 1996 as a lot of work took place to prepare the sanctuary for the annual services. Due to a six week delay in the delivery of the pews and significant work that the general contractor still had to complete, pews were being installed the week before Christmas. As Pastor Bang suggested, members of the congregation were surprised, pleased, and excited by what they beheld on Christmas Eve. The Renovation Committee reported, in the January 1997 *Our Church Paper* that

". . . . Christmas Eve brought the first regular worship services in the refurbished church, and these traditionally impressive and emotional services were particularly moving and exhilarating as a congregation which had seemingly been in exile for over seven months was welcomed back home. . . ."

Congregation members commented positively on how the interior of the church was painted to accentuate architectural detail and how the altar was made free standing with little change to its overall appearance. Congregants also made positive comments about the elegance and beauty of the marble chancel floor, the richness of the refurbished woodwork in the sanctuary, and the improved comfort of the pews. All in all, the congregation of Holy Trinity was very pleased with the results of this challenging project.

Some aspects of the renovation, however, were not yet completed by Christmas Eve, 1996. The revised pulpit, lectern stairs, communion rail, and seating for the choir and clergy were not finished. The Margaret Wendt Organ was not yet playable, so the electronic organ from Redeemer Hall was used instead. In time, these parts of the project would be completed.

In the January 1997 issue of *Our Church Paper*, the Renovation Committee gave many thanks to the Holy Trinity Church staff for their hard work in preparing for Christmas Eve services and for all the extra responsibilities they willingly took on during the whole renovation process. The Renovation Committee cited one individual in particular whose hard work was invaluable during the project:

". . . . Throughout the project, Pastor Bang has found himself in the role of an ad hoc construction supervisor in addition to his more than full-time pastoral duties. Much of the successful outcome of the project is attributable to his daily monitoring of the work. . . ."

On February 9, 1997, a special service was held for the rededication of the newly renovated Holy Trinity

Lutheran Church building and the installation of the Reverend Valerie deCathelineau as assistant pastor. During the service, recognition was given to those who played significant roles in the project, most notably, the Renovation Committee. This group consisted of David Schopp, the chair of the committee, and Dick Bauchle, Jeannette Heiss, Betty Hutcheson, Ronald and Donna Leiser, Cliff Lochhaas, Marty Wright, and the late Carl Kaufmann, who were all committee members. The congregation was commended for its support of the Firm Foundation campaign. The renovation cost $1.5 million – given by the members and friends of Holy Trinity Lutheran Church. The renovation project, which had been central in the life of Holy Trinity Church for two and a half years, was done. Though the Main Street church showed the earmarks of painting, refinishing, and rearranging, the familiar face of the worship space was still evident. The changes to the sanctuary, however, were profound. The altar was moved forward so that the pastors could stand behind it. The congregation would now take communion using movable kneeling rails at the entrance to the chancel. The baptismal font was moved to a new place, and all furniture in the chancel and three congregation pews were made movable to enhance Holy Trinity's concert series. Finally, new pews filled the nave to create a new, yet traditional-looking, worship space. All in all, the renovation project was a big success for Holy Trinity. In his "A Word From The Pastor" column in the February 1997 *Our Church Paper* Pastor Bang looked to the post-renovation era of the Main Street church:

"…. Let's not rededicate our building, let's rededicate ourselves. Let's set our minds and hearts on God and

Christ and the ministry of the Church and the work we
have to do as stewards of God's bounty and kingdom."

After the completion of the renovation, life did not get back to normal; rather, it continued on as usual. The Christian Action Group mounted an in-gathering project creating sewing kits and collecting sweaters all for distribution by Lutheran World Relief. Twenty sewing kits and 160 sweaters would eventually be delivered by Holy Trinity to Lutheran World Relief.

In April 1997, the Holy Trinity Concert Series resumed after a hiatus of almost a year. This first "post-renovation" concert featured the choirs of Holy Trinity and Westminster Presbyterian churches in a benefit for Habitat for Humanity. In the wake of a long and difficult project, the congregation of Holy Trinity continued its traditional mission of helping those in need across the country and the world.

In the spring of 1997, a new ministry was started at Holy Trinity. Proposed by Pastor Valerie deCathelineau, lay communion ministers from the congregation began to distribute Holy Communion to those members who could not attend church. This ministry continues today.

Also that spring, Pastor Bang was chosen to be a delegate to President Bill Clinton's "Summit For America's Future" in Philadelphia, Pennsylvania. He was one of a delegation of ten selected from the city of Buffalo. Congregation President Emerson Horner wrote:

".....Of the many who might have been chosen, it was Charlie who was selected. I was proud to be a member of Holy Trinity....."

On May 4, 1997, the first "Ralph Loew Sunday" in memory of Holy Trinity's fourth pastor took place. To support this event and others like it, The Ralph Loew Fund was established by the Loew family, the congregation, and friends of Holy Trinity. The interest income from this fund would be used to help sponsor speakers and activities on subsequent Ralph Loew Sundays. It should be noted that on this day named for Holy Trinity's pastor emeritus the Reverend Ross MacKenzie, Director of Religion at the Chautauqua Institution, preached at the 10:30 service.

Autumn 1997 came, and with it, the first full Holy Trinity Concert Series since the completion of the renovation. Most notable was the first program in the series featuring the Western New York area premiere of Gustav Mahler's 8th Symphony, also known as "Symphony of a Thousand". The performance of this piece at Holy Trinity involved the Buffalo Philharmonic Orchestra, the Holy Trinity Concert Choir, the 100 voice Choral Union of Houghton College, the newly formed Buffalo Youth Choir, the Western New York Honors Wind Ensemble, 8 vocal soloists, and Holy Trinity's Margaret Wendt Organ. There's no doubt this concert was quite an undertaking!

Later that same autumn, Deborah Bang, wife of Pastor Charles Bang, took a trip to South Africa. Representing the Women of the ELCA, Mrs. Bang spent two weeks in that African nation studying women's concerns and African culture. In February 1998, the Women of the ELCA of Holy Trinity hosted the annual Spring Assembly of WELCA, the Niagara Frontier Conference. Mrs. Bang was the featured speaker at this event and shared the experiences she had traveling in South Africa.

In the winter of 1998, Holy Trinity took yet another

step in its mission to serve its community when the Church Council of the Main Street church voted to become a dues paying member of VOICE, a faith-based community action organization in Buffalo. Holy Trinity joined 23 other urban churches to help with the VOICE mission of revitalizing the city of Buffalo. In the years to follow, a number of Holy Trinity members would become quite prominent in the organization.

Late in the summer of 1998, a new feature was added to Holy Trinity's campus. On the north side of the church's property, a flagpole was erected. On September 13, Holy Trinity observed what was referred to as "Flag Raising Sunday." At the conclusion of the 10:30 service that day, an honor guard assembled by Harold Klein and Richard Hoos led a procession of the choir, clergy, and congregation outside to the grassy knoll between the church and 1092 Main Street. There, the choir offered an anthem based on our national anthem and a new American flag was raised on the new flagpole. A plaque was placed next to the flagpole with the names of those to whom it is dedicated.

The seventh year of Charles Bang's tenure as senior pastor of Holy Trinity came, and with it, a special honor. On May 22, 1999, at the 91st annual commencement exercise of D'Youville College, Pastor Bang was recognized for his work and leadership at Holy Trinity Lutheran Church and for his many activities in various church-related community services.

Pastor Bang was escorted for conferral of an honorary doctoral degree by Stephen C. Ames, a member of the D'Youville College Board of Trustees and a member of Holy Trinity. Sue Ann Wooster Ames, wife of Stephen, read a special citation written for the event. Sister Denise A.

Roche, President of D'Youville, said, when conferring the degree on Holy Trinity's senior pastor:

"We are pleased to honor Reverend Bang for all he has done to help people, his community, and his church, for it is individuals like him that can make a difference in our world....."

Many who know the Reverend Dr. Charles D. Bang would agree that he <u>has</u> made a difference in their lives, the Western New York community, and the world.

The next notable event in the life of Holy Trinity took place on Ralph Loew Sunday, June 13, 1999. On that day, a book of Dr. Loew's memoirs and writings titled *This Faith Tremendous* made its debut. It was compiled by Dr. Loew's wife Maxine and daughters Janet Day and Carolyn Engberg. At the 10:30 a.m. church service, the choir sang a piece written by Dr. Loew, and Pastor Bang crafted his sermon around writings in the new book. After the church service, more than 200 people attended a buffet luncheon followed by a book signing. Mrs. Maxine Loew added her signature to a very special and inspirational collection of her late husband's writings.

In the fall of 1999, Holy Trinity lost one of its most faithful leaders. On November 26, Dr. Kenneth H. Eckert, Sr. died. Dr. Eckhert had served on Holy Trinity's Church Council both as a member and as president during the pastorate of Dr. Ralph Loew. Dr. Eckert also served on a national council of the Lutheran Church in America and played important roles in the planning and building of the Mansperger Chapel and Trinity Tower.

The year 2000 began, and with it, a new millennium.

The English Evangelical Lutheran Church of the Holy Trinity came into this new time with a vibrant congregation full of hope for the future of the parish. Holy Trinity proudly entered its 121st year of witness to the good news of Jesus Christ. In the January 2000 issue of *Our Church Paper*, Pastor Charles Bang put "Y2K" into perspective:

> *"A Word From the Pastor at the Turn of the Century and the Beginning of the New Millenium. . . . As soon as I wrote the heading for this article I realized how powerful those words were. The turn of the century has always prompted plenty of reflection and, with the changing of the millennium, even more. . . . The fact that you're reading this letter, however, means that the world did not come to an end and the Millenium Bug and most Y2K computer problems didn't cause too much havoc for the masses. . . . So what happens next? . . . What will the future hold for us? That's the theme of our prayers on the eve of every New Year; but this year, they seem especially focused. . . . Unless medical science or miracle intervenes in some spectacular way, most if not all of us will not see the turning of the next century; and so there's a secret side of us that wants to remember this one in a special way. We want to have something special to say when people ask, "Where were you when?"*
>
> *. . . . I will be at home with my family . . . not because I'm afraid the lights will go out and the gas lines will cease to deliver, but because I want to be with those who matter the most to me. When someone asks me where I was when – I will say, "With my family." For the remainder of whatever portion of the next century I will live through, when I close my eyes on any night,*

or on my final night, I will have the remembrance of hugging my wife and holding our children when the stroke of midnight came. When our children are old and their grandchildren ask them what they were doing when the next century changed, they will be able to say, "I was in my Mom and Dad's arms in our home in Buffalo."... Pull the camera back a little, and you will see that our little crèche exists within the framework of a larger picture. Pull back farther still and you will see that all of us, all of our existence, all of our lives, indeed all of life, rest in the palm of God's hand. On New Year's Eve, if not for the rest of your life, keep that image in the front of your mind...."

Holy Trinity began the year 2000 by keeping alive its tradition of social activism. The Christian Action Sewing Group announced in January an "in-gathering project" for the new year: to get donations of hand towels and wash cloths for health kits.

In the spring of 2000, planning began for a big event in the life of the Main Street church: Holy Trinity's 125th anniversary in 2004! This celebration would go into 2005 and also celebrate the 100th anniversary of the present sanctuary and the first service held within it.

During the same season, Holy Trinity welcomed a new staff member, a parish nurse named Pat Mohr. Pat offered health advice in *Our Church Paper,* blood pressure screenings, and other health services at Holy Trinity.

In the fall of 2000, a 125th Anniversary Committee was organized and convened, assignments were made, and work on this important milestone celebration began.

During the same autumn, a member was added to the staff of Holy Trinity: Reverend John A. Buerk. Pastor for 28 years of one of Holy Trinity's "daughter" churches, Parkside Lutheran, John Buerk joined the Main Street church as Pastor and Ecumenical Officer. In the December 2000 *Our Church Paper*, he wrote:

> "*...And now I am on a new venture, and I am delighted that this new road leads to where I began in Buffalo – to Holy Trinity. Pastor Bang and I have been friends for years. He is a person whom I respect a great deal. He has intelligence, endurance, a deep faith and a sense of humor. Why, we have even exchanged a joke now and then! ... Thanks for the invitation to join you in this grand enterprise we call the church and its job of loving and caring.*"

On January 14, 2001, Pastor John Buerk, his wife, Jill, and son, Christian, were welcomed to Holy Trinity. Pastor Buerk preached at both the 8:30 a.m. and 10:30 a.m. services, and a reception was held for the Buerk family in Redeemer Hall. During his sermon, Pastor Buerk offered "Ten Ways You Know You're Getting Older." One of them was: "You know you're getting older when you have to lean up against your dresser to pull your socks on ... "

During the winter of 2001, Holy Trinity continued its journey into cyberspace. Kim Koehler, daughter of Bob and Karen Koehler, began working with Pastor Bang to develop a Holy Trinity internet webpage. In time, Kim and her father, Bob, would develop Holy Trinity's own internet website.

In the April 2001 *Our Church Paper*, a questionnaire appeared asking members of Holy Trinity's congregation to indicate whether or not they were interested in a trip to the Luther Lands in Germany as a part of the church's 125th anniversary celebration. The response was very positive. More work associated with the 125th anniversary celebration took place at this time as the History and Archives Committee held three "Archives Nights." During these sessions, the committee began sorting and organizing archival materials that had been stored in various locations around Holy Trinity.

On Sunday September 16, 2001, five days after the terrorist attacks of September 11, Pastors Bang and Buerk offered words of reassurance to the congregation of the Main Street church. In the October 2001 issue of *Our Church Paper*, Pastor Bang offered this eternal truth:

> *". . . God is not silent and has the last word on this, too. These precious ones, these cherished children of God, are not gone forever as those oft repeated images of death and destruction suggest. No, instead they now rest in Him and the witness of the resurrection reminds us that neither life nor death, nor angels, nor principalities, nor things present, nor things to come, nor powers, nor height, nor depth, nor <u>anything</u> else in creation, will be able to separate us from the love of God in Christ Jesus. . . . "*

In late September of 2001, internationally known pianist Earl Wild gave a concert that launched the inaugural season of the Ramsi P. Tick Memorial Concert Series. Conceived by Ramsi Tick, this subscription series of five recitals performed by the world's most acclaimed musicians was originally planned for Kleinhans Music Hall, but, due to production concerns, was moved to Holy Trinity. The Main Street church was home to the Ramsi P. Tick Concert Series through the spring of 2009.

One other event took place in September 2001 that brought sadness to Holy Trinity: The Reverend Dr. Matthew Littleton Winters, senior pastor of Holy Trinity from 1975 until 1992, passed away. Many at the Main Street church fondly remembered Pastor Winters and recalled his ministry, dynamic preaching, and the many contributions he made to Holy Trinity.

In the January 2002 *Our Church Paper*, the new part-time position of Coordinator of Lay Ministries and Pastoral Assistant was added to Holy Trinity's staff. The position entailed keeping a master calendar of all church events and making sure the church paper contained adequate and up-to-date articles and information. Charles Rojek, known to many as "Chuck," was hired to fill the position. One of his first assignments was to help form a men's ministry at Holy Trinity.

The year 2002 was a busy one at Holy Trinity Church. The Social Ministries Committee began to examine the possibility of entering the parish in the Adopt-a-School program. Organist and Choirmaster James Bigham celebrated his 25th anniversary at Holy Trinity. A series of special events were held to commemorate Mr. Bigham's milestone. A coffee hour reception, a formal banquet at the Saturn Club, and a once-in-a-lifetime organ recital featuring four of Mr. Bigham's dearest friends (and most talented organists of our time) comprised the celebration that took place over a three-day period. The 25th anniversary of the Margaret L. Wendt Memorial Organ was also celebrated at this time.

Part Six: The Bang Years — 1992 to the Present

James Bigham, Organist and Choirmaster of Holy Trinity Church.

In the spring of 2002, the 125th Anniversary Committee announced the schedule of major events to take place during the anniversary year. Among these would be the rededication of the church's cornerstone and a banquet and festival service to begin the 125th anniversary celebration. At about the same time, a group of men from Holy Trinity brought together by Chuck Rojek gathered at the Holiday Inn on Delaware Avenue and started a men's group. By mid-June of the year, they would hold their first event: a Father's Day celebration consisting of a coffee hour and a car show. The Father's Day event has since become a tradition at the Main Street church.

Finally, in the spring of 2002, in keeping with its tradition of being a socially conscious church, Holy Trinity presented a program called "Gays and the Lutheran Church." The program attempted to rationally explore and discuss the controversial issues facing gays, lesbians, and churches. It also looked at a recent ELCA Synod resolution concerning this issue.

Planning for and work continued on the 125th anniversary celebration in the summer and fall of 2002. In the fall of the year, another series of archives nights was held at Holy Trinity. Participants in the event, as in the past, gathered for three evenings in a row in Redeemer Hall and sorted through materials and artifacts that had been stored in a room adjacent to the parish hall. The ultimate goal of this process was for the History and Archives Committee of the 125th anniversary to reorganize the material and artifacts into a workable archive.

On Sunday, November 17, 2002, an important goal connected with the 125th anniversary celebration was announced to the congregation by Rudolf L. Bauer, chair of the 125th anniversary celebration. In a temple talk given at both the 8:30 a.m. and 10:30 a.m. services, Mr. Bauer announced a proposed congregational gift of $375,000 to be raised over 125 weeks. The Church Council of Holy Trinity accepted the gift, which would be divided three ways: sums of $125,000 each would go to an Anniversary Mission Fund, an Anniversary Chapel Renovation Fund, and an Anniversary Fund for Debt Elimination. Mr. Bauer's temple talk described the three funds and encouraged members of the congregation to help Holy Trinity to achieve this anniversary goal.

The year 2002 at Holy Trinity was capped off with the Main Street church being one of twelve parishes featured in a WNED-TV documentary titled: "Buffalo's Houses of Worship." The program aired on December 1, 2002 at 8 p.m. It discussed the Buffalo churches from an architectural and aesthetic point of view. Pastor Bang provided some narration for the Holy Trinity segment and some musical accompaniment was provided by Organist James Bigham.

The first events of the 125th anniversary celebration would take place in 2003, beginning with the Main Street church abiding by one of its long-time traditions: The Social Ministries Committee announced that Holy Trinity had adopted Buffalo Public School #82 — an early childhood center located on Easton Street. The first School 82 project was a donation drive for warm hats, mittens, and scarves for the children attending this Buffalo school.

Planning for and projects connected with the 125th anniversary of Holy Trinity continued throughout 2003. In May of the year, work began on a new church directory by co-Chairs of the publication, Chuck and Sue Rojek. Picture taking sessions for the new directory began in August of 2003 and continued into September of the year.

The first "big" event in Holy Trinity's 125th anniversary celebration began on October 3, 2003, when a group of travelers from the Main Street church departed for a tour of the Luther Lands in Germany. Chaired by Pastor John Buerk, the trip was designed around key locations in the life and ministry of the great reformer Martin Luther.

The Holy Trinity tour group arrived in Munich, then visited the Alpine village of Oberammergau, home of the famous "Passion Play" about the life of Christ. The tour group visited Neuschwanstein, King Ludwig's fairytale castle, and then went on to the beautiful medieval towns of Augsburg and Rothenburg.

The tour then took the Holy Trinity group to the German city of Cobourg where they visited St. Moriz Church where Martin Luther preached in 1530. During the same stop, the tour went on to Cobourg Castle and the

Ducal Apartments, Martin Luther's home in 1530.

After visiting Cobourg, the Holy Trinity tour group went on to Eisenach, the location of the Wartburg Castle. It was in this castle that Martin Luther translated the New Testament from Latin into German. On this same stopover, the tour group visited the Bachhaus, Lutherhaus, and Erfurt University, the college where Martin Luther studied.

After the stop in Eisenach, the Holy Trinity tour group then visited the Buchenwald Concentration Camp, then went on to the city of Leipzig. While in Leipzig, the travelers went to the Mendelssohn House and visited Thomaskirche, the church where Johann Sebastian Bach had been choirmaster.

The last two stops on the Holy Trinity anniversary tour were in Wittenberg and Berlin. The tour group from the Main Street church then returned home on October 12, 2003. From all accounts, this tour of the Luther Lands was a great success and was enjoyed by all.

In the same month that the 125th anniversary tour of the Luther Lands took place, preparations were being made for a major project that would take place at Holy Trinity during the anniversary year. Plans for renovation of the Mansperger Chapel were being made, which included the building of a new organ for that sanctuary. In the month of October 2003, a contract was signed in the amount of $267,000 for the construction of a new chapel organ.

In November, another 125th anniversary project was in its developmental stages. When the 125th Anniversary Committee planned Holy Trinity's anniversary celebration, they decided that a special piece of music should be commissioned, composed, and performed during the Main Street church's 125th anniversary year. In November 2003,

Part Six: The Bang Years — 1992 to the Present

the desired composer for the piece of music, Stephen Paulus, came to Buffalo and Holy Trinity for discussions about this aspect of the anniversary celebration.

The second big event in Holy Trinity's 125th anniversary observance took place on December 14, 2003, when the Main Street church celebrated the 100th anniversary of the laying of the cornerstone of the current Holy Trinity sanctuary. Pastor Bang began the 10:30am church service for the third Sunday in Advent on the front steps of the church. He delivered words of remembrance and a rededication of the cornerstone. Ironically, the weather on this day was cold and blustery — similar to conditions 100 years before. Cornerstone Rededication Day continued with a festival service followed by the Annual Congregational Christmas Brunch.

✤ ✤ ✤ ✤ ✤ ✤ ✤ ✤ ✤ ✤ ✤ ✤ ✤ ✤ ✤ ✤ ✤ ✤ ✤ ✤

The 125th Anniversary Celebration of the English Evangelical Lutheran Church of the Holy Trinity

The true beginning of the quasquicentennial celebration of Holy Trinity took place on the weekend of May 1 and 2, 2004. On May 1, a 125th anniversary dinner dance was held at the Buffalo Convention Center to begin the observance of this important milestone in the life of the Main Street church. This event was planned by Deborah Bang, the wife of Holy Trinity's senior pastor.

During the "Opening Litany," a table grace was offered by Pastor Bang that set the tone for the year to come:

" . . . In this time of remembrance we come, O God, as generations before us, to seek your blessing and to speak your praise. We give thanks for those who built this congregation by faith, for those who brought it their hearts' anguish and their souls' rejoicing, for those who sang in it to your glory and those who prayed in it for the sake of others, and for all that teeming life within it whereby we have learned and dreamed and hoped together. Now as we share this meal with one another, may we remember that meal of bread and wine through which we are offered the gifts of heaven and around which we gather each week and in its partaking, be given a glimpse of your eternal kingdom here on earth . . . Amen."

Following this table grace, the more than 200 people who attended this event enjoyed a meal of Sliced Tenderloin of Beef, Chicken Wellington, or a vegetarian entrée of a Grilled Marinated Portabella Mushroom. After dinner, a program of remembrances, tributes, and music was enjoyed by all in attendance. Remarks of remembrance were given by Dr. Mary Botsford, granddaughter of Holy Trinity's second pastor, Frederick Kahler, Jill Schleifer-Schneggenberger, and Brittany Beard. Two special tributes were also given this particular evening. The first was to honor Pastor John Buerk on the occasion of the 45th anniversary of his ordination into the Ministry of Word and Sacrament. This tribute was given by Pastor Charles Bang. Another brief tribute was given to 125th anniversary Chair Rudolf Bauer and his wife Julia on the occasion of their 50th wedding anniversary. This tribute was given by celebration hosts Ronald Pellnat and Deborah Bang.

After the program of remembrances and tributes, all

Part Six: The Bang Years — 1992 to the Present

in attendance enjoyed lively conversation and danced to the music of an eight-member band named "Orengue." The following day, Sunday, May 2, a "Festival Service of Holy Communion in Celebration of the Quasquicentennial of the English Evangelical Lutheran Church of the Holy Trinity" was held at 10:30 a.m. Preservice music was performed by organist James Bigham and the Holy Trinity Choir.

The festival service began with Pastor Bang offering a prayer of dedication at the entrance of the church:

"Brothers and Sisters. We have come together to celebrate the 125ᵗʰ anniversary of the founding of this congregation to the glory of God. For 125 years it has been a place for the worship of Almighty God and for the building up of the body of Christ. We ask your blessing this day on these your faithful servants and upon all those who will enter into this sanctuary from this day forward, that it may continue to be a place for the gathering of the people of God, a place for proclaiming the Gospel through Word and Sacrament and a place for bringing life and hope to us and to this community. Thanks be to God!"

Following this prayer, the festival procession took place to Hymn 548 in "The Lutheran Book of Worship":

"Oh, worship the King
all glorious above,
Oh, gratefully sing
His pow'r and his love;
Our shield and defender
the Ancient of Days,

Pavilioned in splendor,
and girded with praise."

During the service, prayers of rededication were
offered at the lectern and pulpit, the baptismal font, and the
altar. The service concluded with a prayer of rededication of
the people of God:

"Blessed are you, O Lord our God, King of the Universe.
The heavens and the earth cannot contain you, yet you
are willing to make your home in human hearts. We
are the temple of your presence and this building is the
house of your Church. Accept us and this place to which
we come to share with others the covenant you make
through Holy Baptism to praise your name, to receive
your forgiveness, to hear your Word and to be nourished
by the body and blood of your Son. Be present always
to guide and illumine your people. And now, O God,
visit us with your mercy and blessing as we rededicate
ourselves to your glory and honor and the service of all
people. . . . "

The next event in Holy Trinity's anniversary celebration
took place on May 9, 2004. This was Ralph Loew Sunday
with guest speaker, Dr. Richard Carlson of the Lutheran
Theological Seminary in Gettysburg, Pennsylvania. On
May 30, 2004, six eighth graders were confirmed at Holy
Trinity. A special anniversary event marked this occasion
known as "Confirmation Reunion Sunday". Former Holy
Trinity confirmands gathered at the 10:30 service and were
given recognition for having reaffirmed their baptism at the
Main Street church.

Also in May, an "Anniversary Scroll" was placed in the church for all members of the congregation to sign. It was on display for the duration of the anniversary celebration.

On June 6, 2004, Holy Trinity held a 125th Anniversary Ice Cream Social after the 10:30 service. This event was held for members of Holy Trinity's "daughter" churches.

During the spring of 2004, a number of former assistant pastors and interns who had served at Holy Trinity returned to the pulpit of the Main Street church to preach as a part of the anniversary celebration. This program continued throughout the year. By the end of 2005, more than a dozen former pastors and interns reunited with the church that had played an important role in the formative days of their ministries.

In the June 2004 issue of *Our Church Paper*, Pastor Bang offered these words about Holy Trinity's 125th anniversary:

"I suspect our heavenly Father smiles as He looks back on our birthday in 1879 ... and says, "How can this be?" ... I suspect He also looks at us, all these years later, and sees how we have grown and matured, how beautiful we have become, how much we have accomplished, and how we have tried to make our positive mark on the ledger of creation, and says, "Congratulations!" ... "

While Holy Trinity's anniversary celebration was getting underway, projects were going on around the church. During the spring and summer of 2004, renovations of the sacristy and the choir studio took place. The work in these areas of the building would be completed in the fall of 2004.

During the same summer, the property at 23 North Street was reverted to Holy Trinity ownership, and the building was emptied and cleaned.

On September 5, 2004, the Holy Trinity chapel closed for its renovation to begin. Removal of pews and the chapel organ took place, new lighting was installed, and paint samples were reviewed. The old chapel pews that were removed were made available to church members for a $100 donation to the 125th Anniversary Fund.

"Rally Day" took place on September 19, and with it, a special celebration planned by the Christian Education Committee. Following the 10:30 a.m. service, an old-fashioned picnic lunch took place in the Holy Trinity staff parking area behind the chapel complex consisting of hot dogs, hamburgers, clowns, face painting, an inflated playhouse, and entertainment provided by the Nickel City Road Show. This event was well attended and enjoyed by all – especially the children of Holy Trinity.

A week after the 125th anniversary "Rally Day" celebration, the last Sunday of September 2004 was dedicated to a remembrance of Frederick Kahler who was pastor of Holy Trinity from 1884 until 1927. Pastor Bang gave a special sermon on this day dedicated to the life and ministry of Dr. Kahler, and a luncheon followed the service with a number of Dr. Kahler's descendants in attendance. In the weeks to come, Sundays with special sermons by Pastor Bang would be dedicated to Henry Pflum, Ralph Loew, and Matthew Winters, all of whom served Holy Trinity Lutheran Church as senior pastors.

The fall of 2004 continued to be busy at the Main Street church. On Reformation Day, October 31, Mrs. Elizabeth Winters and her family returned to Holy Trinity

Part Six: The Bang Years — 1992 to the Present

to commemorate "Pastor Matt Winters Day." On November 14, the bell tower in front of the Mansperger Chapel complex was rededicated, and the November 2004 issue of *Our Church Paper* announced that the church paper itself was now available on the internet via a link on Holy Trinity's website. One hundred and thirteen years after its creation, *Our Church Paper* was now in cyberspace!

On December 12, 2004, Holy Trinity's annual Christmas pageant was staged. A special anniversary moment was added to this program where those in attendance who had appeared in a previous Holy Trinity Christmas pageant were invited to come forward and join the current cast in the singing of "Silent Night." Between cast members and pageant "alumni," the whole area in front of the first row of pews was filled with people from one side of the church to the other! Also on this day, the rededication of Trinity Tower was celebrated.

While all these anniversary activities went on during the fall of 2004, the Main Street church continued to display its giving character by continuing the School 82 project. The Social Ministries Committee continued to collect and deliver school supplies and collected money to be put toward the construction of supply carts for the school. Richard Butz of Holy Trinity's Men's Group and his technology class at Buffalo State College built the supply carts. Julia Bauer and her committee contributed by making over 500 chair pockets for the backs of the students' chairs. The hand sewn pockets were made to hold the very school supplies collected at Holy Trinity.

The first half of the 125th anniversary culminated on Christmas Eve with the debut of the original musical composition which had been commissioned by the Main Street church for this celebration. Titled "Calm on the

Listening Ear of Night," the choral piece consisted of an 18th century poem by Edward Sears set to music written by Stephen Paulus.

As planned, Holy Trinity's chapel, without a new organ, was reopened by Christmas and a Christmas Day service took place there. The chapel was rededicated on January 23, 2005 in a series of services held in that sanctuary.

Six days later, a major music event took place at Holy Trinity. Staged in the main sanctuary of the church, a 125th anniversary concert was given involving the Holy Trinity Chancel Choir, organist James Bigham, and the Buffalo Philharmonic Orchestra. During the performance, Holy Trinity's new Steinway grand piano, given in memory of Gerri Schleifer-Schneggenburger by her family and friends, was dedicated.

The 125th anniversary concert culminated with the specially commissioned piece by Stephen Paulus being performed again — this time by Holy Trinity's choir, Mr. Bigham, and the Buffalo Philharmonic. In addition to a larger production of Stephen Paulus' composition, the composer was in attendance to hear the orchestral debut of his work. This concert was well attended, very well received, and quite memorable!

The next big event in Holy Trinity's 125th anniversary celebration occurred on February 13, 2005. Known as "Wedding Reunion Sunday," couples who were married at Holy Trinity were invited to come back to the parish where their nuptials took place and reaffirm their wedding vows at the 10:30 a.m. service. Before the church service took place, husbands and wives were asked to assemble in order to process into the main sanctuary. The turnout for this event was so great that the lineup of couples stretched

The 125th Anniversary Committee of Holy Trinity in 2005.
First row: Donna Leiser, Martin Bauer, Anniversary Chair Rudolf L.
Bauer, and Janet Day. Second row: Helen Wright, Sue Rojek, and Linda
Schmidt. Third row: Reverend John A. Buerk, Charles Rojek, Ronald
Leiser and Reverend Charles D. Bang.

from the foot of the stairs leading up to the narthex all the way through Redeemer Hall to the rear entrance of the Fireside Room!

The renewal of vows ceremony took place after the collection of the offering and the choir anthem. Pastor Bang asked the couples who had processed into the church to stand and face each other. At this time, marriage vows were reaffirmed by numerous voices choked with emotion. A pronouncement was made by Pastor Bang that was followed by a lot of kisses, hugs, and many tears. This was a very moving and meaningful celebration at the Main Street church.

In the final two months of Holy Trinity's 125th anniversary celebration, more guest preachers who had been associated with the Main Street church as pastors or interns returned to their former parish, and a hymn fest took place. Then, on May 1, 2005, Holy Trinity's 125th anniversary celebration came to a close.

On this particular day, the Sixth Sunday of Easter and "Ralph Loew Sunday", words of appreciation for those who planned the 125th anniversary celebration were offered during both the 8:30 a.m. and 10:30 a.m. services. Both worship services ended with the same well-known hymn:

"Now thank we all our God
With hearts and hands and voices,
Who wondrous things has done,
In whom his world rejoices;
Who, from our mothers arms,
Has blest us on our way
With countless gifts of love
And still is ours today."

LBW Hymn 534

After the 10:30 a.m. service, a "Thank You" brunch brought the 125th anniversary observance to a close. During this event, anniversary Chairman Rudolf Bauer and his committee were recognized for the work they did to make this celebration a great success. It had truly been a memorable year in the life of the Main Street church.

❖ ❖ ❖ ❖ ❖ ❖ ❖ ❖ ❖ ❖ ❖ ❖ ❖ ❖ ❖ ❖ ❖ ❖ ❖ ❖

Much has happened at the English Evangelical Lutheran Church of the Holy Trinity in Buffalo, New York, since May 1, 2005. First, the 125th anniversary gift goal was not only met but exceeded by the family and friends of the Main Street church.

In the period since the anniversary celebration, Holy Trinity parted with two of its properties adjacent to the church. 49 Linwood Avenue, which had been the parsonage, the vicarage, and the residence of Otto and Lilli Rosin, was sold, as well as the WNED property at 23 North Street.

On January 29, 2006, the dedication of the Rev. Dr. Ralph William Loew Memorial Organ in the Mansperger Chapel took place. The new chapel organ, built by Kegg Organ Builders of Uniontown, Ohio in 2005, made its debut in a special concert given by organist James Bigham and Holy Trinity's Chapel Choir. In the summer of 2006, the bell tower in front of the Mansperger Chapel, and the roof of the church were repaired and restored.

In the spring of 2007, Rev. Eric Olaf Olsen of New York City was extended a call to become a pastor at Holy Trinity. Pastor Olsen gave a powerful audition sermon, accepted the call given to him by Holy Trinity's congregation and was installed as pastor on October 28, 2007. Pastors Bang and Buerk had major roles in the ceremony.

One other change in the church staff took place in 2007. Carol Trost retired from her position as parish secretary after 25 years of service to Holy Trinity. Linda Lipczynski was then hired to be the new parish secretary. James Bigham, also celebrated his 30th anniversary as Organist and Choirmaster of the Main Street church.

Another project was begun in the winter of 2007 with the renovation of Redeemer Hall. The first part of this task involved the complete revamping of the heating system followed by installation of new lighting, block glass windows, and the refurbishing of the area under the narthex. In 2008, the Ladies' Room adjacent to Redeemer Hall and the Fireside Room was also renovated.

In the autumn of 2008, Holy Trinity entered into an exciting new partnership with one of its former "daughter" parishes, Parkside Lutheran Church. After the pastor of Parkside Lutheran resigned to accept a call in Canada, Pastors Bang and Olsen accepted a call to step in and help the vacant Buffalo parish. The main effect of this association is that one of Holy Trinity's pastors conducted the 9 a.m. service at Parkside Lutheran on Sunday mornings. Activities between both the Holy Trinity and Parkside churches took place to create fellowship between the two congregations. It should be noted that Rev. John Buerk also participated in the "Parkside Project," preaching at the church where he was given the title "Pastor Emeritus" after serving 28 years there as senior pastor.

Also, in the fall of 2008, Holy Trinity entered into another relationship – that of being a sponsor of a refugee family from the nation of Rwanda. Rev. Jean Baptiste Twagirayesu-Uwimana, his wife, Kezie, and their five children were welcomed at Holy Trinity and provided a home in the city of Buffalo. The Social Ministries Committee coordinated this effort – the third such sponsorship in the church's history. Previous sponsoring of refugee families at Holy Trinity took place in 1976 and 1981. The Twagirayesu-Uwimana family became members of Holy Trinity in May of 2009—part of a class of 40 new members!

On Reformation Sunday, October 26, 2008, a great celebration occurred. Planned months in advance by a "Super Secret Anniversary Team," the congregation of the Main Street church celebrated the 25th anniversary of the installation of the Rev. Dr. Charles D. Bang as pastor of Holy Trinity. This was a surprise event which unfolded during the processional hymn at the 10:30 a.m. service. As

Part Six: The Bang Years — 1992 to the Present

Pastor Bang and his wife Deborah

Pastor Bang, in his usual place in the procession, approached the pews near the front of the sanctuary, he saw his daughter, Sarah, embraced her, and the celebration was off and running. Unbeknownst to Pastor Bang, his daughters Katie and Sarah both came home for this celebration.

Several special guest participants played important roles in Pastor Bang's 25th anniversary celebration. Bishop Marie C. Jerge of the Upstate New York Synod of the Evangelical Lutheran Church in America led Pastor Bang and the congregation through a renewal of the promises he made during his installation 25 years earlier. The Rev. Carol E. A. Fryer, who had been an intern at Holy Trinity when Pastor Bang was beginning his ministry at the Main Street church, shared fond recollections of her colleague, and Father Jacob Ledwon of St. Joseph University Roman Catholic Church, a dear friend of Pastor Bang, delivered the sermon.

Pastor Bang and his wife, Deborah, were presented a gift from the congregation by Congregation President Paul Bauchle, and the celebratory service was followed by a reception in Redeemer Hall. As Pastor Bang would say, it was "a great day" in the life of Holy Trinity! The "Super Secret 25th Anniversary Committee" of David Parks, Paul Bauchle, Lynn Glieco, Charmaine Kaltrider, and Pastor Eric Olsen was given thanks for coordinating a great event — and keeping a secret so well!

As always, music played an important role in this celebration. Organist James Bigham and both the Chancel and Chapel choirs of Holy Trinity performed preservice music on the occasion of Pastor Bang's 25th anniversary and offered many wonderful musical moments during the festival Reformation Sunday service.

In April of 2009, Pastors Bang and Olsen prepared yet another celebration – that of the 50th anniversary of the ordination of Rev. John A. Buerk as a pastor in the Evangelical Lutheran Church in America. Pastor Buerk delivered a special sermon in church on Sunday, May 24, and was given a coffee hour in his honor that day. On Wednesday, May 27, 2009, fifty years to the day of his ordination, Pastor Buerk was honored at a gala banquet at the Saturn Club of Buffalo. At this event, many tributes were paid to him and the impact of his ministry.

It's at this moment that the story of the first 130 years in the history of Holy Trinity comes to a close. The end of this book is but a pause, though, in the life of the cathedral of Lutheranism in Western New York. As these words reach this page, the next chapter in Holy Trinity's life is being written, and though faces may change in the sanctuary, the spirit stays the same. The Rev. Dr. Ralph Loew characterized Holy Trinity best in his closing remarks in *This Faith Tremendous*, the book that chronicled this parish's first hundred years:

". . . .This church is a supportive fellowship insisting on the redeeming, forgiving, loving, growing, rejoicing possibilities in discovering the love of Jesus Christ. . . . "

These words still ring true thirty years after they were

written. And in this age where so much changes so fast, the English Evangelical Lutheran Church of the Holy Trinity is a symbol of that which is unchanging: God's eternal love. The building at 1080 Main Street is a monument to a steadfast faith, a faith that created a congregation and built an enduring house of worship. That passionate faith is alive and thriving today and continues to spread the good news of the Gospel far beyond its own walls. Holy Trinity Lutheran Church stands fast....and will for many years to come.

"Were they to take our house,
Goods, honor, child, or spouse,
Though life be wrenched away
They cannot win the day.
The Kingdom's ours forever!"

Martin Luther, "A Mighty Fortress is Our God"
LBW Hymn 229

✠ ✠

Made in the USA
Charleston, SC
13 July 2013